AFTER A THOUSAND TEARS

A publication of the
Stuart A. Rose Manuscript,
Archives, and Rare Book Library
at Emory University

 EMORY
UNIVERSITY

FOUNDING EDITOR
Pellom McDaniels III

SERIES EDITOR
Clinton R. Fluker

AFTER
A THOUSAND
TEARS

POEMS BY

Georgia Douglas Johnson

FOREWORD BY Maureen Honey

NEW INTRODUCTION BY Jimmy Worthy II

ORIGINAL INTRODUCTION BY Cedric Dover

The University of Georgia Press ⚓ Athens

© 2023 by the University of Georgia Press
Athens, Georgia 30602
www.ugapress.org
All rights reserved
Designed by Melissa Buchanan
Set in Garamond Premier Pro and Transat
Printed and bound by Integrated Books International

The paper in this book meets the guidelines for
permanence and durability of the Committee on
Production Guidelines for Book Longevity of the
Council on Library Resources.

Most University of Georgia Press titles are
available from popular e-book vendors.

Printed in the United States of America

23 24 25 26 27 C 5 4 3 2 1

Library of Congress Cataloging-in-Publication Data
Names: Johnson, Georgia Douglas, 1886–1966, author. | Honey, Maureen, 1945–
writer of foreword. | Worthy, Jimmy, II, writer of introduction.
| Dover, Cedric. writer of introduction.
Title: After a thousand tears : poems / by Georgia Douglas Johnson ;
foreword by Maureen Honey ; new introduction by Jimmy Worthy II ;
original introduction by Cedric Dover.
Description: Athens : The University of Georgia Press, [2023]
| Series: Stuart A. Rose Manuscript, Archives, and Rare Book Library at
Emory University Publications | Includes bibliographical references.
Identifiers: LCCN 2022042430 | ISBN 9780820362830 (hardback) |
ISBN 9780820362847 (epub) | ISBN 9780820363608 (pdf)
Subjects: LCGFT: Poetry.
Classification: LCC PS3519.O253 A69 2023 |
DDC 811/.52—dc23/eng/20220914
LC record available at https://lccn.loc.gov/2022042430

FOR GEORGIA

CONTENTS

↯

AFTER A THOUSAND TEARS

I. THE HEART OF A WOMAN

II. AMBERGRIS TO GALL

III. NOR THIS, NOR THAT

IV. WITH LEVEL LOOK

V. THE GULF OF CHALLENGE

FOREWORD

Maureen Honey

The last collection of poetry Georgia Douglas Johnson published appeared in 1962. It was her fourth book, but the first three, appearing at the height of the Harlem Renaissance, had already established Johnson as that iconic era's foremost woman poet. Johnson's achievement is highlighted by the fact that very few African American women were able to publish a collection of verse in the early twentieth century despite their prominence in New Negro anthologies and journals. Johnson's female peers included a host of superb poets, such as Alice Dunbar-Nelson, Angelina Weld Grimké, Gwendolyn B. Bennett, Helene Johnson, Jessie Redmon Fauset, and Anne Spencer, yet none of them were able to publish an edition of poetry, nor does their published oeuvre in their lifetimes amount to more than a few dozen poems each. In contrast, Johnson published well over two hundred poems over the course of her very long life, and she never gave up hope that her unpublished work would see the light of day even as she entered her eighty-eighth and final year.

Now sixty years after her fourth collection appeared, a fifth volume of this amazingly prolific and dominant poet's verse appears on the scene, edited by Dr. Jimmy Worthy II. It's the most significant publication of Johnson's writing since Claudia Tate's comprehensive compilation of her work in 1997. Worthy recovered *After a Thousand Tears: A Negro Woman's Verse*, as the collection was originally titled, from the papers of Anglo-Indian writer Cedric Dover, which are housed at Emory University, deposited there in 2009. As Worthy makes clear in his splendid introduction, if it weren't for

Dover's preservation efforts and his vast library, this fifth and largest of Johnson's poetry collections would likely have been lost. *After a Thousand Tears* adds 81 poems (although a few appeared earlier) to the 142 pieces that appeared in *The Heart of a Woman and Other Poems* (1918), *Bronze: A Book of Verse* (1922), *An Autumn Love Cycle* (1928), and *Share My World* (1962).

Worthy's meticulous research reveals that this volume came into existence during World War II, and it sheds new light on Johnson's creative life in the 1940s, a decade by which she and her sister and brother poets had mostly stopped being published. He walks us through Johnson's correspondence and close friendship with Harold Jackman during these years when she tells Jackman she had submitted *Tears* for review to an unidentified editor at the end of 1944. He also describes its subsequent 1947 scheduled release by Padma Press of Bombay with Dover's introduction. It never appeared, but Dover saved the manuscript he brought to Padma, which is what we have before us in a remarkable resurrection heralded by Johnson herself in her poetic meditations on intimacy, aging, death, war, resistance to racism, and hope for the ultimate establishment of multiracial worldwide harmony. All of these topics are brought together in *After a Thousand Tears*, showcasing Johnson's vast range: lyrics that celebrate fleeting passion, unflinching accounts of aging and heartbreaking loss, poems of pride in mixed-race identities, praise for the battle-worn courage of Black men fighting for the race's survival, and a final statement of hope, unity, peace, and humanity's common ground. It's as if Johnson wanted to bring together her lifelong writing on these topics in the many genres at which she excelled and to do so in the one that defined her: poetry.

Worthy's capacious contextualizing of *Tears* in his introduction is a welcome explication of Georgia Douglas Johnson's complexity and her poetry's continuing relevance to readers today. Deceptively simple and brief, these pieces, he says, amount to "discursive veiling, a mode of literary subterfuge whereby romantic poetry appears to endorse the age's masculinist preoccupations while undermining the assumptions on which such gender conventions rest." Johnson's feminism has long been recognized by scholars, but Worthy pries open how deftly she subverted the New Negro call for women to "mother the race" and perform middle-class notions of domestic femininity. He here joins Akasha Gloria Hull, Claudia Tate, Cheryl A. Wall, Nina Miller, and others in highlighting the African American woman writer's central challenge: how to be a New Negro woman activist/artist within a masculine paradigm fashioned by the movement's largely male architects.

In his perceptive reading of two of her best-known poems, "The Heart of a Woman" (1918) and "Wishes" (1927), along with several others, Worthy persuasively argues that Johnson's "poetic persona envisioned modes of freedom deemed socially unacceptable." Specifically, the speaker in these signature poems undermines the heteronormative domestic sphere of marriage as an inhibiting boundary for her soaring spirit, her desire to fly high and free herself from confining definitions of femininity. She yearns for the freedom to be herself, immersed in the moment, for the freedom to go wherever she chooses. The irony of Johnson's being praised as feminine and representative of the New Negro woman's respectability when she is actually expressing "subversive yearning" is on clear display in these poems, according to Worthy, who says this 1947 volume recalls but intensifies her previous poetry's "furtive critiques" of conventional gender roles.

Johnson was not alone in creating such a persona, as several scholars of the period have noted, but she was certainly the most prolific and public, having her poetry endorsed by some of the biggest leaders of the New Negro Movement: William Stanley Braithwaite, W. E .B. Du Bois, Alain Locke, and James Weldon Johnson. Worthy unpacks the comments of each in their forewords to her collections and, in the case of JWJ, his influential anthology *The Book of American Negro Poetry* (1922, 1931). We see how carefully Georgia Douglas Johnson navigated the centrality of Black manhood and female domestic virtue to these intellectuals' agendas while earning their respect for her lyrical vision, advancement of the movement's goals, and ability to command readers' attention with pithy condensation of her clear-eyed observations.

The clearest way her subversive yearning is on display, in my view, is when Worthy describes the close friendship Johnson had with gay, lesbian, and bisexual writers through her correspondence with them and the Saturday night salons she hosted at her Washington, D.C., home during the 1920s. Langston Hughes, Bruce Nugent, Harold Jackman, Wallace Thurman, Mary P. Burrill, Alice Dunbar-Nelson, and Angelina Weld Grimké, among others, were regular visitors at these weekly gatherings, and some, like Jackman, stayed in her orbit long after the Harlem Renaissance was over. As Worthy asserts, she mentored these artists, gave them a home away from home, literally nourished them, and was inspired by them to explore her own transgressive feelings and experiences. Worthy uses Johnson's friendships with these artists as a springboard for new readings of her well-known "Escape" (1925) and "Wishes" (1927), interpretations that foreground the poems' erotic conceptions of death expressed in startling vaginal imagery. I found similar erotic imagery in Angelina Grimké's meditations on death in poems from the 1920s, and framing Johnson as a kindred spirit opens up a new understanding of her modern sensibility.

Like Grimké, Bennett, Dunbar-Nelson, Fauset, and other major New Negro women poets, Johnson hid her personal life from public view, well aware of her role as a model of Negro womanhood cutting through salacious stereotypes of Black women. Yet all of them wrote verse reflecting heartache, despair, unattainable love, erotic transport, and yearning for a world beyond the one they were given. We've been able to reconstruct much of their private lives through letters, diaries, unpublished memoirs, and accounts by people who knew them well through papers they left to universities and various archives. For Georgia Douglas Johnson, however, we have fewer resources despite her "Catalogue" of unpublished work housed in her longtime home at 1461 S Street NW. Most of it tragically was thrown out on her death, with the remainder housed in her archive at Atlanta University and Howard University. Yet as Claudia Tate and Akasha Gloria Hull have shown, it's possible to glimpse the life behind the curtain so as to illuminate the joy and anguish expressed in her poetry. Although more biographical work needs to be done to flesh out the woman behind the poetry, this recovered collection allows us to see more of this poet's fertile imagination and to have evidence of her continued productivity well beyond the Harlem Renaissance.

Not only did Johnson outpublish her female peers, she did so after getting a late start, unlike many poets of the 1920s. Johnson's first collection appeared when she was forty-one and her last the year she turned eighty-five. The year *Tears* was scheduled to be released, 1947, she turned seventy. What struck me with the greatest force in this recovered volume was part 2, "Ambergris to Gall," which consists of sixteen poems that present unflinching portraits of a woman aging as Johnson approached that milestone. Even today, it's hard for writers to speak forthrightly about getting old and facing their mortality, yet Johnson created speakers who state squarely the price they pay for getting to live a long time, the awareness of how much they've lost as time marches on and of their inevitable end point at the grave. "One lives too long: / The days grow pale / And never-ending grow the nights— / One lives too long" ("One Lives Too Long"); "I look into my glass— / Who is this woman old and grey / With lips so pale, I pray?" ("Hokku"); "There's a time in the heart of a woman / When she comes to the end of the road, /

When life has hushed its joyous song / And hope is a heavy load" ("Heartbreak Age").

Johnson left us searing statements about how it feels to grow older, to be without a lover or companion, to see one's beauty fade and become invisible, to realize that, in the end, we face our disappearance pretty much on our own. She didn't pull any punches, nor did she turn away from the hard stuff as she challenged her readers to withstand life's fiercest blows, whether from vicious racists, faithless lovers, disillusionment, the fleeting nature of happiness, or the pain of being a forgotten star, a fallen dreamer. She put the anguish out there plain as day, in direct language accessible to readers then and now. *After a Thousand Tears* is well titled. It presents those tears as a life force shed by speakers who open their hearts and share what's inside them with the world, who are alive enough to have produced a thousand tears but not so weakened by them that they drown.

As Worthy so eloquently states in his praise of Johnson's final poem in the collection, "Resolution," "Although this poem foreshadows her death in 1966, its delight in the animating core self who resists decline suggests that her poetry serves as autobiographical testament to her most fervent yearnings." He tells us we're left with "an image of resurrection," the vision of a restored world, and the dream of knowing a free self in harmony with a unified unprejudiced human race. That we need such a statement of hope in our current era is self-evident, and to have Georgia Douglas Johnson be its posthumous deliverer affirms her sorely tested belief in the power of love to transform, not only ourselves but our fallen world. This recovered rich text is a gift for which I and others are profoundly grateful.

ACKNOWLEDGMENTS

The completion of this project would not have been possible without the boundless support of Monique Worthy, Betty Worthy, Jimmy Worthy III, Autumn Worthy, Charlotte Wilborn, and Christopher Wilborn. I would also like to thank Judith L. Stephens for her friendship as well as her personal and professional encouragement throughout the life of this project. For her scholarship, support, and availability to write the foreword to *After A Thousand Tears*, I am grateful to Maureen Honey. Thank you also to Ronald Dorris and Mark A. Sanders for their friendship and vision. I am also appreciative for the wonderful assistance provided by librarians and archivist at Emory University's Stuart A. Rose Manuscript, Archives, and Rare Book Library (particularly Courtney Chartier, Rachel Detzler, and Carrie E. Hintz); Howard University's Moorland-Spingarn Research Center; the Schomburg Center for Research in Black Culture; the University of Massachusetts, Amherst's Special Collections and University Archives; and the Atlanta University Center Robert W. Woodruff Library. Thank you to Stephen McGinty, the interim subject librarian for the English Department at the University of Massachusetts, Amherst, for directing me to a wealth of materials published by Padma Publications of Bombay throughout the 1940s. Special thanks to my colleagues Nick Bromell and Caroline Yang for their critical eyes and generous spirits. I am also appreciative to Patrick Allen, acquisitions editor at the University of Georgia Press, not only for believing in the necessity of restoring Georgia Douglas Johnson's poetic voice in *Tears*, but for his kindness and patience, as my opportunities to research were severely curtailed during the pandemic. For their unparalleled scholarship and dedication to African American women's interiority as expressed in creative genius, I am profoundly grateful to Claudia Tate, Cheryl A. Wall, Barbara Christian, Akasha Gloria Hull, Maureen Honey, Judith L. Stephens, Hazel V. Carby, Ajuan Maria Mance, Elizabeth McHenry, and Erin D. Chapman. Lastly, I am appreciative for the funding I received in support of my work. I want to thank the Massachusetts Society of Professors and the Dean's Office at the University of Massachusetts, Amherst (particularly Barbara Krauthamer and Joye Bowman), for granting Research Support funds. I am grateful to have been awarded from the Rose Library the Nancy and Randall Burkett Fellowship for Research in Black Print Culture, an award that made possible a more acute study of the conventions and historical contexts Johnson navigated. Thank you also to Provost Anne McCall and the Office of Academic Affairs at Xavier University of Louisiana for awarding Faculty Research Support Funds.

DISCURSIVE VEILING AND
THE REIMAGINED WORLDS OF
GEORGIA DOUGLAS JOHNSON

Jimmy Worthy II

When read alongside a critical evaluation of the New Negro Movement, Alfred Lord Tennyson's poem "Ring Out, Wild Bells" (1850) serves as an apt reflection of the movement's engendering ideals and glaring shortcomings. Heralding psychic and spiritual restoration that is to attend new commitments to morality and justice, the speaker's proclamation to "Ring in the thousand years of Peace" is made possible by the individual and national implications of ringing out "a slowly dying cause," and thus, adherence to the unprogressive, destabilizing ethos of the fleeting moment. To the extent to which the sound of Tennyson's ringing bells will signal new and old, reclamation and ruin, the speaker fails to offer an interpretive mode for distinguishing opposite signals that sound the same.

The Crisis featured two stanzas of "Ring Out, Wild Bells" on the January 1919 cover, and inside, W. E. B. Du Bois's editorial located in this Victorian poem's central contradiction an analogy for the frustrations of claiming Black, citizen patriotism in the early twentieth century. He laments, while "all Europe rejoices in its new gifts—the British proletariat is promised a liberal labor program," the joy of nationalism for Czechoslovakians, liberation in France, and recovery in Belgium—"*our* men, who have helped mightily to awaken and preserve the spirit which makes these things possible, are returning to what?"[1] In other words, the metaphoric bell ringing as a sign of renewal and advancement for Europe only emphasized the familiar ring of virulent racism manifesting in attenuated citizenship for African Americans. Endorsed in the pages of Charles S. Johnson's *Opportunity*, Alain Locke's *The New Negro*, and James Weldon Johnson's *The Book of American Negro Poetry*, Du Bois's rejoinder to second-class citizenship and the perception of African Americans' ill suitability for full participation in the modern world reflected the masculinist tone of the movement: "we black Americans must fight, must push forward. . . . We must do combat on our own Western Front." That such a decidedly political and masculinist proscription for racial advancement was reiterated during the flowering of African American artistic production deprioritized Black women's lived experiences and literary accomplishments.

Generally reviewed favorably by scholars who lived through the Harlem Renaissance, romantic, or genteel, poetry written by women was interpreted as attesting to the race's respectability and heteronormative social adherence by implicitly refuting Black "mis-speakers" bereft of humanity portrayed in nineteenth- and early twentieth-century dialect writing and minstrel shows. Women's poetry, then, offered a "supporting role" to the prevailing agenda reinforced by later critics who deemed such poetry superfluous to the racial advancement expressed in more strident calls for political transformation. Women's lyric poetry ostensibly reflective of its authors' genteel, bourgeois femininity not only reified the New Negro as self-assured, sophisticated male determiner but purportedly projected "that the race could most fully participate in a libidinally charged national culture and identity."[2] "The New Negro," as Locke would argue, "must be seen in the perspective of a New World, and especially of a New America."[3] The images and creative impulses of African American women were not to win them "their own self-determination but to assist black men in the effort to achieve theirs."[4] Thus, as Black women rang in the New Negro's "spiritual coming of age" made possible by their artistry and activism, they heard in their marginalization claims of stasis and regression that could be mitigated by circumscribing their fulfillment within the gender conventions of the new age.

When placed in its historical context, poetry written by women during the Harlem Renaissance evidences the first modern Black female voices. As Maureen Honey contends, rather than suffering from an imitative impulse, such poetry is animated by a "defiant sensibility reflective of the rebellious women who wrote it."[5] As a rebellious woman whose lyric poetry expressed, in Akasha Gloria Hull's phrase, "quiet sedition," Georgia Douglas Johnson employs a modernist imagination to furtively critique expectations of exemplary Black femininity and the self-negation that often accompanied the performative drive to "mother the race."[6] Perhaps it is unsurprising then that the title of an unpublished volume of poetry by Johnson appropriates Tennyson's declaration, "Ring in the thousand years of peace," to provoke reassessment of the ideologies, fantasies, and erasures undergirding restorative aspirations. *After a Thousand Tears: A Negro Women's Verse*, as it was originally titled, represents the only extant poetry collection that Johnson authored between 1928 and 1962. Correspondences with Harold Jackman between 1938 and 1944 suggest that she composed *Tears* during these years and submitted the collection for review on December 25, 1944.[7] How her poetry was received and the name of the editor to which she sent *Tears* remain mysteries. In Padma Publications of Bombay, Johnson would secure a publisher who prepared the book for release in 1947.[8]

Described by Padma as "a distillation ... of a rich personality, typical of liberal thought throughout the coloured world," the poetry in *Tears* is arranged into five sections: "The Heart of a Woman"; "Ambergris to Gall"; "Nor This, nor That"; "With Level Look"; and "The Gulf of Challenge." As we will see, Johnson—as with New Negro poets Angelina Weld Grimké, Alice Dunbar-Nelson, Gwendolyn B. Bennet, Anne Spencer, and others—participates in strategic masking, or what I term discursive veiling, a mode of literary subterfuge whereby romantic poetry appears to endorse the age's masculinist preoccupations while undermining the assumptions on which such gender conventions rest. Johnson's critique of social structures that ultimately prove ruinous to individual fulfillment finds further expression in poems addressing race and romantic entanglements as sustaining sources of the imagination. In *Tears*, then, Johnson adheres to many of the themes that characterize her poetry in earlier collections, but she intensifies her furtive critiques.[9] With varying assessments, Cedric Dover identifies these themes in his introduction, "One Life Full Certified." Moreover, that *Tears* celebrates refutation to established power relations codified in law and reified in social practice may have assisted Padma's readers who contemplated liberated personhood after the passage of the Indian Independence Act of 1947.[10] Thus, although composed well after the New Negro Movement, in *Tears* Johnson invokes a poetic persona whose transgressive preoccupations not only retrospectively indict gender conventions relative to the expectations assigned African American women during the movement but also envision performances of freedom usable to a contemporary, international audience. Ostensibly well timed for its 1947 release, Padma chose not to publish the collection for reasons not known.

It is to Cedric Dover that we most owe appreciation for the book's preservation. The bibliophile and race theorist kept Padma's mock-up of *Tears* and stored it in his extensive library. When Dover's papers were deposited in Emory University's Stuart A. Rose Manuscript, Archives, and Rare Book Library in 2009, Johnson's volume was also archived. If Dover had not have saved *Tears*, it is quite probable that the volume would have remained lost. Owen Dodson recorded the means by which additional works were lost when immediately following Johnson's funeral in 1966, he observed the treatment they received:

I do know that she had a great deal of unpublished material—novels, poems, essays, memoirs, remembrances, all kinds of things. But as the car stopped in front of her house, the men were cleaning out the cellar, and I clearly saw manuscripts thrown into the garbage. I said, "A lifetime to the sanitation department!"[11]

That Johnson's fourth poetry collection survived as part of Dover's library rather than her own offers tragic and ironic commentary on the disinterest in preserving works of the most prolific woman writer of the Harlem Renaissance. May Miller Sullivan, Johnson's close friend who, as Johnson lay dying, sat at her bedside stroking her hand and repeating quietly, "Poet Georgia Douglas Johnson," unsuccessfully beseeched Johnson's son, Henry Jr., "to preserve the barrels of papers that his mother kept at home."[12] As Judith L. Stephens notes, we are fortunate that in November 1992 (twenty-six years after Johnson's death) Karen L. Jefferson and Joellen El-Bashir, both of Howard University's Moorland-Spingarn Research Center, rescued "many of Johnson's papers that remained in her former home at 1461 S Street NW, Washington, D.C., before it was to be renovated and sold."[13] Among the retrieved typescripts, correspondences, fragments of unpublished works, unpublished poetry, photographs, and newspaper clippings that eventually filled seven boxes was Johnson's "Catalogue of Writings," a directory listing, with brief descriptions, the books, plays, poetry, short stories, and songs for which she was unable to find publishers. Johnson deposited her "Catalogue" in the archive at Atlanta University "either in 1963 when she attended the Baccalaureate Services or in 1965 when she returned to her alma mater to receive the honorary degree Doctor of Letters."[14]

Yet, Johnson does not list *Tears* in the "Catalogue." Nor does the directory fully account for the voluminous writing she references in letters written to Jackman and Dover between 1944 and 1947.[15]

Assessing the totality of Johnson's literary sensibility is not only strained by the incomplete record of unpublished materials but also by her penchant for pseudonymous writing.[16] Addressing Johnson's use of various nom de plumes, Alice Dunbar-Nelson wrote in her As in a Looking Glass column of May 13, 1927, that "Georgia Douglas Johnson has as many aliases as Lon Chaney had faces. One is always stumbling upon another nom de plume of hers."[17] Indeed, using the pen name John Temple, she won first prize in the *Opportunity* contest for her play *Plumes*. She would adopt the alias Paul Tremaine in 1936 and 1937 respectively to publish "Gesture" and "Tramp Love," two stories that reflect the sexual fluidity and geographic mobility often denied Black women.[18] Thus, Johnson's aliases announced a fictionalized identity that could articulate in direct and exploratory ways themes unsupported by Black respectability politics. Furthermore, as Claudia Tate argues, Johnson was "fully convinced, and rightly so, that her readers would be more likely to treat her works seriously if she disassociated her black and female self from them."[19] Writing as a man, then, disburdened her of the responsibility of race and gender identity, thus freeing her to further express a complex interiority.

Given the context of Johnson's publication record, that *Tears* survived (and with her own name) is remarkable, particularly given that the poetry it contains suggests her dissatisfaction with claiming a subversive voice at the expense of her Black, female identity defined and performed on her own terms. For if we are to observe seriously Johnson's artistic imperatives in *Tears*, we must maintain a critical lens that does not separate her posture as "lady poet" and salon hostess from her substantive critiques of social arrangements that obscure and champion hierarchical values. Suturing what appear as competing agendas centralizes her modernist imagination and allows for clearer readings of how she marshals tropes of subversion to disrupt prevailing ideologies. In *Tears*, then, Johnson

participates in a revision of romantic, gender, religious, and ulti-
mately existential tenets by critiquing and re-creating a world suf-
fering in male fantasy. This recovered volume of poetry confirms
what Erlene Stetson theorizes in her reading of Johnson's first vol-
ume, *The Heart of a Woman* (1918), that her poetic persona is pre-
occupied with destroying such fantasy.[20]

Contextualizing Johnson's life relative to the two literary eras that
most inform her artistic sensibilities evidences the gender norms
circumscribing her identity and her capacity to resist these struc-
tures through creative pronouncements. Georgia Douglas Johnson
(née Camp) was born in 1877 to biracial parents in Atlanta, Geor-
gia.[21] She attended public schools in Atlanta and in 1893 completed
her studies at Atlanta University's Normal School. Johnson then
taught school in Marietta, Georgia, before resigning to attend the
Oberlin Conservatory of Music. She would later reveal that she
"dreamed of being a composer" before she turned to poetry "and
put her songs away" when "the words took fire and the music
smouldered."[22] Yet I suspect that she discovered in romantic po-
etry, particularly poetry that invokes the "lyric moment," a useful
mode through which to render her lived experiences as a collection
of moments suffused with emotional intensity that "escape time
and the social contract."[23] Johnson's biographical sketch in *Car-
oling Dusk* attests to the implications of poetic form, particularly
the poetics of William Stanley Braithwaite.[24] After returning to
Atlanta in 1903, where she worked as a local assistant principal, she
married Henry Lincoln Johnson in the same year. The possibility of
escaping the strictures of Black elite society and Victorian feminine
performance by expressing her creative impulses would prove indis-
pensable when she and her husband, along with their two children,
Henry Lincoln Johnson Jr. (1906–1990) and Peter Douglas John-
son (1907–1957), relocated to Washington, D.C., in 1910.[25]

In 1912 President Taft appointed Henry Lincoln Johnson to a four-year term as recorder of deeds, securing the Johnsons an elevated social status that surely necessitated stricter adherence to the postemancipation gender norms African Americans adopted between 1865 and the First World War. These beliefs and patterned performances were conspicuous refutations to Black idiocy and subhumanity rendered in late nineteenth-century "local color" literature. A genre that strategically combined realism and romance to celebrate regional specificity, "local color" transformed southern romance into a national literature, helping to generalize and make creditable depictions of subservient, loyal, trustworthy Black dependents who, along with their former white, benevolent caregivers, mourned the simplicity of social relations eradicated by emancipation. Creating nostalgia for a time that never existed, images of African Americans in "local color" "served to ally anxieties over lingering sectional strife and over the effects of industrialization on the 'New South.'"[26] Other forms of American popular culture, particularly the minstrel stage, relied heavily on the assumption of Black intellectual vacancy. Performers whose faces were darkened with burnt cork "dramatized the buffoonery of black being in language, costume, and pose."[27] Representations of African Americans who were essentially performing their own feeble Black being evidenced the absence of complex interiority and the absurdity of African American existence absent of a white supremacist overseer who could manage their overdetermined instincts. Informed by seventeenth- and eighteenth-century English poets, African American poets including Frances Ellen Watkins Harper (1825–1911) and William Stanley Braithwaite (1878–1962) rejected popular depictions of Blackness by adopting the romantic tradition. These poets contrasted the ubiquitous image of Black misspeaking with literature that incorporated elevated diction, symbolism, and metaphor. Their embrace of the romantic tradition was also a claim to middle-class, bourgeois society, signaling the capacity for betterment through socioeconomic upward mobility.[28]

To be certain, poets and writers who adapted dialect speech for counterhegemonic purposes, Paul Laurence Dunbar (1872–1906) and Charles Chesnutt (1858–1932) perhaps chief among them, created personae and characters whose "broken English" concealed trickster intentions. Thus, literary works of this type demonstrated the absurdity of Black intellectual deficiency. Yet by modeling behaviors in accordance with gender conventions representative of middle-class American society, the romantic tradition offered African Americans a way to marry the politics of poetics with the politics of social posture. In a historical moment replete with images of inherently licentious African Americans ruled by emotion and instinct, accepting Western cultural norms complemented the aims of romantic poetry. In direct contradiction to Blackness as sign of primitive status, African American male leaders, particularly in the last decade of the nineteenth century, embraced the ideology of "separate spheres." Accordingly, Black women's domestic work was designated "private" and in opposition to Black men's struggle for civil rights in the "public" sphere. As African Americans experienced the most visible forms of racial prejudice in the "public" sphere—judicial, legislative, commercial, political—Black men's struggle "was conceptualized as a gendered offensive to make a plea for black manhood within a social order that sought to limit the exercise of male power . . . to those men who were white."[29] Thus, while African American women and men were both responsible for advancing the race, the struggle for civil rights became understood as operating within African American men's purview.[30] Ajuan Maria Mance argues that as a result of this uplift strategy of social parity, poetry written by Black women that depicted the events and conditions of Black women's lives "either undermined or was irrelevant to the larger struggle for racial justice."[31]

Ironically, postbellum, pre–New Negro poetry written by Black women at one time lauded for its counternarrative qualities was now a liability that threatened individual and collective respectability as the race prepared to enter the twentieth century. That beliefs in the supposed superfluous nature of Black women's poetry extended well into the 1930s meant that early twentieth-century African American women were advised to "mother the race" through domestic duties and support of fraternal organizations or embody, what Nina Miller terms, the "exalted Negro Woman."[32] Even as women such as Elise Johnson McDougald assumed that women were better responsive to the welfare of the race by attending to domestic duties and Black patriarchal organizations, she admits that under these limiting conditions the Black woman "knows little peace and happiness."[33] Certainly blues women's participation in the sex-race marketplace actualized their vision of identity dislocated from stilted, Black feminine performance.[34] Yet for Georgia Douglas Johnson and other women poets of the New Negro era, successful negotiation of the publication arena often meant endorsing a particular masculinist reality or arrangement of male aspirations in poems that did not obviously account for their own subjectivities. While the young Turks, Langston Hughes and Claude McKay in particular, had the relative freedom to address the political implications of racial exclusion—thus complementing the Black self-determination agendas championed by James Weldon Johnson, A. Phillip Randolph, and Marcus Garvey—women poets especially were constrained by the imperative for propaganda.

In "The Criteria of Negro Art," Du Bois maps the means by which art as propaganda would elevate the race, but he does not address the Black male restorative project undergirding this strategy of persuasion.[35] Such strategy was informed by modernist thought also in social currency. Modernist thought not only interpreted

African Americans as "primitive"—exotic, emotional beings who would "rescue the West from the grips of a calculating, materialistic, reason-bound 'Nordic' civilization"—but consistently prefigured the "primitive" as a feminized being.[36] Therefore, the effort to efface their own feminization led Black male thinkers and artists to champion an overdetermined portrait of feminine virtues. Ironically, then, Black women's subjugation in art and society was constitutive of the race's, and their own, improvement. Indeed, in his introduction to *The New Negro*, Locke designates "the negro" male and having emerged from a feminized and infantilized position of dependence to take his place as an integral member of American society.[37] Obviously, African American men did not subscribe to a homogenous vision of manhood or theoretical claim to it, but reoccurring signals throughout the New Negro Movement show a propensity for imitating sexist practices on display in the broader culture. Therefore, writing while also confronting inherited gender protocols circumscribed Georgia Douglas Johnson's creative output as much as her social world. She and her three books of poetry published between 1918 and 1928 could be praised for exemplifying feminine virtues that did not threaten a Black masculine prerogative.[38]

Accordingly, in *The Book of American Negro Poetry* (1922), James Weldon Johnson extols her "ingenuously wrought verses" composed with "sheer simplicity and spontaneousness," while suggesting that her "verse possesses effectiveness precisely because it is at the pole opposite to adroitness, sophistication, and a jejune pretention to metaphysics."[39] Weldon Johnson "appreciates her verse by regarding it not as art but as natural, transparent, feminine, self-expression, in contrast to" the "cultivated artistic creation" of masculine expression.[40] Likewise, in his foreword to *Bronze*, W. E. B. Du Bois declares Johnson's poetry "singularly sincere and true" and revealing "of the soul struggle of the women of a race," while in his recommendation written on Johnson's behalf to the Guggenheim Memorial Fellowship Foundation, he regards her "erratic, illogical, and forgetful." Echoing Weldon Johnson's reading of her natural spontaneity, Du Bois concludes, "she is liable at any time or anywhere to turn out some little thing of unusual value and beauty," insisting that Johnson "could never do a concentrated, sustained piece of work."[41] For Johnson to have been identified as "the foremost woman poet of the race," "the lady-poet," or simply as a poet may very well have necessitated her adherence to romantic poetics and genteel femininity that could be interpreted as acceptance of masculinist uplift strategy. Thus, her outward social projection, when aligned with her poetic sensibility, declares her visible and attests to her commodified status. Yet, as Marita Bonner suggests, the choice to exist within cultural and artistic conventions was not determinative of African American women's interior life, nor did it preclude subversive actions and ideas intended to disrupt the very beliefs to which they purportedly subscribed.[42]

Written accounts of Johnson's public life portray tendencies for convention. As Johnson's attire was representative of her feminine comportment, so too was the responsibility she claimed as host of her Saturday night salons.[43] Occurring regularly in the living room of her home from about 1921 to 1928, then sporadically into the 1930s, these Saturday night literary gatherings, as Elizabeth McHenry documents, created "a society through which the most prominent literary and intellectual minds of the 1920s, as well as lesser luminaries of the decade, passed."[44] Johnson's home, which she referred to as "Half-way House," offered respite and the promise of intellectual stimulation for those traveling through and living in Washington, D.C. Individuals Johnson arranged became a supportive community whose intellectual engagement and creative pronouncements resisted African American object status. Finding Washington, D.C., generally devoid of encouragement for young African American poets and playwrights, Langston Hughes remembers himself and other writers coming to "Halfway House" "to eat Mrs. Johnson's cake and drink her wine and talk poetry and books and plays."[45] The hosting duties to which Hughes refers allowed Johnson to maintain the expectations of bourgeois femininity, while also fostering creative exchange and critical discourse that she would need to further her own creative imagination. As we will see further when reviewing the poetry in *Tears*, Johnson developed her own strategy of protective cloaking wherein she uses the outwardly claimed role to effect creative and personal freedoms. This is not to argue that she was without personal investment in post-Victorian gender conventions and their attendant cultural representations, but it is to posit that in her social etiquette she overemphasizes these conventions to challenge the limitations she faced.

Geraldyn Dismond's *Pittsburgh Courier* column further calls attention to Johnson's public displays of traditional femininity, and thus her protective cloaking. Dismond divulges that before meeting Johnson and because of the "place she [Johnson] occupies in the Negro Renaissance," "I had expected to see a brusque, cold-blooded individual whose efficiency and belief in sex equality would be fairly jumping at one." That Johnson was not "engrossed in herself and work, sophisticated and self-sufficient," but was instead "very sensitive, retiring and absolutely feminine" meant that her feminine posture could mitigate the masculine implications of her renaissance participation.[46] When economic restraint during the Depression and Johnson's fatigue from working outside of the home after her husband's death in 1925 contributed to the literary society's demise, she continued to employ what Dismond saw as a particular feminine performance to nurture younger writers and explore suppressed desires. In her frequent correspondence with gay and lesbian writers—during and well after the Saturday nighters era—who often addressed her as "mother," Johnson could embrace a maternal role while finding kindred spirits with those whose sexual orientation resisted heteronormative constraints.[47] Indeed, while the surrogate mother role she embraced portrayed her more as godmother than artist who furtively critiqued, Johnson's fondness for those who transgressed social propriety was reflective of her own contrarian desires. If she found in the sexual freedom and self-defining personhood of her "children" the means to access the deeper wells of subjectivity, this insight would further contextualize the affairs she seems to have had. Correspondences between Johnson and W. E. B. Du Bois suggests that the two had an affair that predated and continued after Henry Lincoln Sr.'s death. In a letter Du Bois wrote from Moscow in 1926, he informs Johnson, "I am thinking of you. I'd like to have you here." He then requests that she "Please come down half dressed with pretty stockings. I shall kiss you."[48]

While Johnson's public life illustrates her preoccupation with convention, private reflections and her own writing evidence subversive yearning. Alice Dunbar-Nelson suspects an affair as the source of Johnson's poetic inspiration in *An Autumn Love Cycle*.[49] Moreover, the three sonnets she wrote to Angelina Weld Grimké, Alain Locke's conclusion that the poetry in *Autumn* evidences Johnson "rediscovering the Sapphic cult of love," and her own pseudonymous description of herself as the combination of Sappho and "the nun-like Miriam" not only suggest that she may have held same-sex attraction but also that her poetic persona envisioned modes of freedom deemed socially unacceptable.[50] Beyond illustrating the capacity to read with greater complexity Johnson's gender and sexual identities, however, her poetry also exhibits strategic refutation to ideologies rooted in essentialist arguments. We find an example of such poetry in her most anthologized poem, "The Heart of a Woman," a work that further demonstrates her concealed inclination for subversion:

The heart of a woman goes forth with dawn,
As a lone bird, soft winging, so restlessly on,
Afar o'er life's turrets and vales does it roam
In the wake of those echoes the heart calls home.

The heart of a woman falls back with the night,
And enters some alien cage in its plight,
And tries to forget it has dreamed of the stars
While it breaks, breaks, breaks on the sheltering bars.[51]

Scholars have correctly assessed this poem as Johnson articulating the pronounced challenges that attend Black female personhood in the early twentieth century. Indeed, Johnson's poetic persona employs the metaphor of a bird in flight to describe women's naturally unrestricted, liberated core and the particularly damning effects of caged existence, even behind "sheltering bars." Yet she seems to do more than place in opposition women's authentic desires and institutions or beliefs that confine the self. If, as Johnson suggests, a woman's heart is the epicenter of animating interiority, then she portrays this space as provoking pleasurable and imaginative flight, while countering this description by declaring that the calls to return home—the place presented as unnatural cage—emanate from the same source. In this way, the persona seems to present as equally natural unbridled imagination and the curtailing of these regenerative experiences by desiring to return home. That the persona transitions from the natural desire to return home to depicting the home as "alien," and thus unnatural and confining, does not indict the home as a space intended to reify traditional gender performance. Rather, the persona suggests the woman as fundamentally flawed for finding home oppressive, therefore guilty of exhibiting unnatural, unwomanly instincts.

Rather than using "The Heart of A Woman" to endorse gender restriction, however, Johnson uses this poem to invalidate essentialist readings of Black women's desires that are inflected by the "natural" urge to maintain patriarchal expectations. For if women find unnourishing the "natural" return to oppressive spaces, Johnson suggests the problem lies not in Black women but with the essentialist formula that prefigures them destined for confinement and domesticity. Furthermore, as Johnson implicitly rebuffs notions of innate limitation, she collapses the restrictive categories circumscribing the lives of African American women and men. Read as an example of romantic poetry reflective of the author's refined sensibility and disposition for convincing the broader culture of Black and white similarities, "The Heart of A Woman" challenges racist assumptions that African American women *and* men confront. Thus, while interpreted as attuned only to women's interior lives, Johnson's implicit critique further questions Black writers and intellectuals' rejection and acceptance of particular essentialist formulations. As resistance to white supremacist ideologies was increasingly coded as Black men's aesthetic and political terrain, Johnson conceals an argument against inherent Black inferiority and the adaptation of these beliefs in Black patriarchal spaces within a call to expand the opportunities for Black women's self-expression. According to Maureen Honey, these efforts of indirection and code register the complex intersection of gender, race, and oppression evident throughout women's poetry of the Harlem Renaissance.[52]

These efforts also refute the notion that Johnson addressed race as theme in poetry primarily as a response to Locke's and Du Bois's criticism of the "nonracial" nature of poetry in her first collection, *The Heart of a Woman*. However, she does seem to admit disinterest in incorporating racial themes into poetry. In a letter to Arna Bontemps, she admits, "Whenever I can, I forget my special call to sorrow and live as happily as I may. Perhaps that is why I seldom write racially. . . . But, lest we forget, we must now and then come down to earth, accept the yoke and help draw the load."[53] Scholars have interpreted Johnson's revelation as proof of a general disinclination for composing racial poetry. Yet I posit that Johnson's comments reflect rejection of a particular discourse surrounding Blackness that disconnects women's interiority from examinations of Black identity. In light of her propensity to conceal and the various ways "The Heart of A Woman" signifies as gender and racial critique, the burden she describes more aptly identifies the social responsibility of addressing race in ways only congruent with bourgeois expectations. Johnson's poetic sensibility often presents readings relative to racial identity that arise directly from Black women's lived experiences with suppressed selfhood and the means to redress such oppression. The load she is to help draw, then, is not race but rather an interpretation of Blackness that obscures the relationship between race and Black women's interior life. Although *Bronze*, her collection of racial verse, represents Johnson bending to the social pressure engendered by Locke's and Du Bois's criticism, in her "nonracial" poetry she makes possible the promulgation of conventional beliefs while promoting "self-affirmation through the individuality that could be expressed in lyric poetry."[54] In this way, her position as woman and artist not completely post-Victorian or New Negro works to her benefit.

Johnson's personal and creative investment in disrupting racist beliefs and the sexist assumptions foregrounding a masculinist uplift strategy show that she practices what Keith D. Leonard describes as self-naming, and thus the capacity to effect liberation by redefining the characteristics, commitments, values, and identities signifying womanhood.[55] In its cover and poetry, *Tears* exemplifies this orientation, not only functioning to further challenge the restrictive and supremacist formulations evident in her "racial" and "nonracial" poetry, but also to at times extend this critique to propose the creation of a new society unbound by gender and racial hierarchies.

The cover to *Tears* features an incomplete, hand-drawn picture of an older woman with eyes cast downward and a slightly tilted head, as her body faces to the right. This drawing bears striking resemblance to the picture of Johnson drawn and printed in a B. J. Brimmer Company advertisement for *Bronze*. On the advertisement, Johnson is drawn as a younger woman emerging from shadow that covers part of her face and body. As with the woman on the cover of *Tears*, Johnson faces to the right, but her eyes look forward confidently. Although the picture of Johnson portrays her wearing an open neckline blouse or dress, her décolletage is absent of cleavage, inviting future readers of *Bronze* to associate her racial poetry with modest femininity. While it appears that the artist intended to draw the woman of *Tears* wearing the same attire, the woman's clearly arched eyebrow, pronounced lip color, and exaggerated eyelashes suggest that she also claims a performance of femininity at odds with Johnson's, perhaps looking down as she laments the age at which she finally projects sexuality and self-expression. Indeed, the woman possesses a self-regulated feminine identity that acknowledges her modesty and sensuality. That dispassionate reserve and bold self-assertion characterize her gender identity, however, suggests that the woman could be read as projecting not conviction but apprehension, issuing from the challenge to maintain traditional feminine respectability and youthful beauty standards. Therefore, readers might interpret the downcast eyes as symbolizing the difficulty and complexity of claiming femininity as an older woman. The shadow on the woman's face and neck that begins to envelop her, then, heightens the figure's ambiguity, as the darkness could signal consuming gender regulations, veiled desires, or a protective space that an age-registering light cannot penetrate.

When compared with the advertisement's picture of Johnson, the woman on the cover of *Tears* appears to represent Johnson and her preoccupations in 1947. Further validating this conclusion, Johnson may have drawn the woman as a self-portrait. Because the design on the cover of *An Autumn Love Cycle* was drawn from a sketch by Renaissance poet Effie Lee Newsholme (Newsome), Akasha Gloria Hull wonders "if GDJ herself was the artist who adapted it."[56] Therefore, Johnson could have similarly drawn a more age-appropriate version of herself using the advertisement's image as the basis for her revision. In this way, the ambiguity operating in the picture of the older Johnson casts Johnson as an artist who intentionally incorporates obfuscation in her design. Such rhetorical gesture not only plays with readers' expectations for the poetry in *Tears*, it further evidences Johnson's capacity to manipulate the aesthetics of convention and transgression so that readers engage or anticipate Johnson's subversive messaging when viewing her image. In line with Braithwaite—whose introduction to *The Heart of a Woman* suggests, then retreats, from the possibility that Johnson's verse expresses the "deeply human"—Dover's introduction fails to fully account for the complexity Johnson brings to the cover and poetry in *Tears*.[57]

Titled "One Life Full Certified," Dover's introduction is an earlier draft of "The Importance of Georgia Douglas Johnson," his tribute to Johnson published in the December 1952 issue of *The Crisis*. He regards *Tears* as a "sifting of her collected work" that is "lit by the glow of a rich, mellow personality . . . typical of cultivated thought in a large part of the coloured world." Dover then appears to acknowledge Johnson's style of masking subversive critique, identifying the sections "The Heart of a Woman" and "Ambergris to Gall" as concealing within the "chords of conventional familiarity" commitments to pleasure and the "continued joy of being alive." According to Dover, rather than rehearsing themes of "undying devotion" and "the usual regrets of the passing years" that coalesce into "uniform greyness," these two sections chant a carpe diem resolve, amounting to singing "the pleasures of loving today and sorrowing, if needs be, tomorrow." Yet Dover trivializes this astute portrait by foregrounding a reductive assessment of much of the poetry in Johnson's first three collections, echoing Du Bois's and Locke's criticism. He praises *The Heart of a Woman* for its "fine sensibility," then faults the collection for failing to champion the explicit political agenda he reads in "Claude McKay's moving sonnets of protest." After celebrating McKay's departure from "conventional poetising," Dover interprets the subject of *Bronze* as "the heart of a coloured woman, but now ... aware of her social problem and the potentiality of the hybrid."[58] Thus, Dover not only makes women's interiority and Black lived experience distinct categories, he defines the nature of such experience narrowly and suggests that the value of *Bronze* lies in its thematic proximity to *Harlem Shadows*.

He maintains this separation when assessing *An Autumn Love Cycle*, concluding that in place of "enlarging the new vitality" present in *Bronze*, *Autumn* reverts to the personal notes of *Heart*, "with the aching maturity of a sensitive woman in her forties." Tellingly, Dover does not simply miss the ways in which Johnson's "nonracial" poetry in *Heart*, *Autumn*, and *Tears* encompass neglected Black, female realities, he regards the exploration of women's interiority as an impediment to the more significant work of overtly refuting white supremacist social structures. Indeed, the "circumstance of being a Negro" apparently saves Johnson from the inability to find creative outlet in a "transitional society." Rather than paralyzed by an unprogressive, gender-inflicted poetic yield, Johnson's racially based identification with suffering sustains her and her relevance, as it also "rouses a passionate belief . . . in ultimate justice and the coming brotherhood of man."[59] As Nico Slate contends, "Dover focused on attacking racism and imperialism, without sufficiently recognizing their intersection with gender inequality."[60] This orientation motivates Dover to insist that in *Autumn* Johnson is "again overcome by herself," before lauding her "courage, persistence and intuitive understanding" reflected in poetry addressing biraciality.[61] Johnson's "nonracial" poetry, then, becomes a manifestation of selfish gender indulgence set against her capacity to employ intuition and racial solidarity to promote collective redemption.

The first two sections of poetry in *Tears* dispute Dover's assessment by identifying the counterhegemonic potentiality of Black women's imagination and freedom quest. "A Song" exemplifies this process, evoking time, memory, and creative pleasure to problematize and resolve burdened, female existence:

> She sang....
>
> Surrendered years came trooping through my heart,
> Freighted with tears and laughter, joy and pain;
> I stood at April, starry-eyed, and then—
> Ran down the gamut of my life again!

The persona hears this woman bear witness and truth in a voice that transmits into sound the lyrics of her life's story. That previous years of the woman's life were surrendered and now return weighted with emotional autonomy stresses the expectation for sacrificed desires and the psychic injury that attends this gender convention. Spontaneously restored from the space of suppression, the years bring with their reappearance the opportunity to finally lament their passage and lost possibilities. However, the singer also confronts the occasion to absolve herself of such agony, standing on the precipice of April, or renewal, idealistically anticipating the years she will claim as her own. Yet the singer now rejects expectations, declaring that she, "Ran down the gamut of my life again!" Her choice to engage years lost to sacrifice is not only a choice to embrace abandoned joys and pains, but it also signals the decision to, in Ralph Ellison's often-quoted examination of jazz, "keep the painful details and episodes of a brutal experience alive in one's aching consciousness, to finger its jagged grain, and to transcend it."[62] Thus, Johnson offers a jazz singer who discovers in her reclaimed experiences and through her voice inevitable solace that engenders psychic freedom. More than an accomplishment, this freedom functions as a conceptual space of regeneration separating her from a reality saturated with sexist and racist ideologies. The conceptual space Johnson creates, then, is one of radical self-care, and thus, as Audre Lorde posits, a domain of self-preservation and political warfare.[63]

In "Wishes," Johnson enlarges the symbolic register of this space. Although "Wishes" was previously published in 1927, when read alongside "A Song" the persona details another way to access imagined geographies of liberation. Similar to the persona's flight in "The Heart of a Woman," the journey depicted in "Wishes" nourishes the mind's desire for freedom. Fatigued by "pacing the petty round / Of the ring of the thing I know," the persona turns her attention from "the ring," or symbol of matrimony and its attendant patriarchal values, to actualizing the yearning to explore areas separate from the domestic realm. By first proclaiming, "I want to stand on the daylight's edge / And see where the sunsets go," she signals curiosity that can only be satiated with her own eyes, but more significantly, she signals the connection between sunset and fulfillment. Indeed, the majority of the persona's journey occurs in partial or total darkness, thus connecting sex-based restriction and respectability politics to an oppressive daylight. Echoing Langston Hughes's poem "Dream Variations," the persona manifests in her unconfined movements the joys of exploration unburdened by evaluative gaze. Sailing through the liberating, personhood-inducing dark expanse, she affirms this space as another terrain of self-preservation.

Yet in the poem's last two lines, the persona transitions from this image of flight and divulges a seemingly counterproductive

Book ad for *Bronze*.
Stuart A. Rose Manuscript,
Archives, and Rare Book
Library, Emory University.

Georgia Douglas Johnson
author of
Bronze: A Book of Verse
with an introduction by
WILLIAM E. B. DU BOIS
PUBLISHED BY
B. J. BRIMMER COMPANY
79 MYRTLE STREET   BOSTON, 14, MASS.

solution to her daytime plight that omits the function of night.
Johnson writes, "I want to keep all the tears I weep / And sail to
some unknown place." Cheryl Wall concludes that this last im-
age "underscores the extent of the speaker's current confinement,"
even as the nature of that confinement and the cause of her tears
remain undefined.[64] I contend, however, that Johnson, through her
persona, evokes tears to again undermine the conventional notion
that women's emotionality serves to indicate weakness that re-
quires male strength for complement and correction.[65] In line with
the dual representation of tears present in Johnson's poem "Tears
and Kisses," the tears in "Wishes" indict daylight ideologies, but
they also become a transportive substance that she produces which

enable her to access a restorative space with an unknown location. This space, then, is an elevated version of the one she figures earlier in the poem, deriving its power to regenerate from its secret location, and thus its total anonymity from the daylight world. As the last lines appear to confirm gender stereotype, they furtively critique inherited beliefs while describing the means by which women might use their sorrow to inhabit a safe place that perpetually sustains subjectivity.

Restorative darkness and the secret space find further coherence in the persona's beckoning for shadows to envelope her. "Escape" illustrates this insistence as Johnson merges resistant darkness and the protective realm, bringing her prescription for women's radical departure from "daylight" to its highest form:

> Shadows, shadows,
> Hug me round
> So that I shall not be found
> By sorrow.
> She pursues me
> Everywhere,
> I can't lose her
> Anywhere.
> Fold me in your black
> Abyss,
> She will never
> Look in this.
> Shadows, shadows,
> Hug me round
> In your solitude
> Profound.

That the persona calls for darkness to conceal her from a female-personified sorrow suggests that the psychic injury evident in "A Song" produced a bifurcated consciousness whereby the self divided between embracing and opposing daylight ideologies. Sorrow's constant pursuit of the speaker who looks to shield herself from threatening influence exposes a contentious power dynamic that the persona recognizes darkness can resolve. Yet this form of darkness differs from the sunless sky in "Wishes," as it not only guards against the loss of personhood but also surrounds the persona with incredible solitude. The vast depth of solitude and Blackness that characterize the abyss act as descriptors for a space suggestive of death. If the area characterized in "Escape" serves as metaphor for restorative death, then the persona must enter this realm to receive necessary protection. That she requests to be folded into this space that will continually hug her round indicates death's embracing nature, and it establishes erotic binding between death and the persona. Just as she reveals that "the gift of death / Is merciful—when understood," her connection with death attests to deeper understanding.[66]

Perhaps just as significant, the persona's erotic attachment to death suggests that she prioritizes this connection above those with heterosexual partners. Indeed, that death has the capacity to fold her into its dark opening is suggestive of female anatomy, whereby vaginal folds, or labia majora and minora, cover the vaginal opening. Thus, in the accomplishment of accessing the hospitable "dark opening," the persona enjoys a lesbian relationship with death, one that nourishes the core self while simultaneously further undermining the necessity for fulfillment only through heterosexual union. Moreover, because the tears in "Wishes" enable entrance into the secret, "unknown place," the persona makes from those tears vaginal lubrication that offers unchallenging movement into death's body. The repurposing of tears in this way deepens the symbolic implications of the collection's title, *After a Thousand Tears*. Because the persona derives protection and pleasure from sexual contact with death, sorrow's search for her will prove fruitless, as this figure of respectability would never enter death's body. Therefore, as the personified withers, the persona's consciousness is made whole again.

Affirming that love from another cannot replicate death's liberating and pleasure-inducing presence, the persona either erases the love interest from particular poems or yokes the promise of love to a time-restrictive, predatory daylight. In "Hokku," for example, following the presentation of traditional tropes of female longing, the persona creates an unsurpassable gulf between her and the love interest, effectively omitting him from her heart: "For refuge, I might marry you, / But 'twould be treason to my heart . . . / It would be lonely." In "The Day Is Fleet," however, she both erases the love interest and exposes the relationship between daylight and love's promise. This poem is a revision of "Amour," published in *Autumn*. Johnson not only renames this poem—attaching the characteristic of abrupt to day—but she also omits the love interest from "Amour." Whereas erotic encounter with the love interest inaugurates the persona's quest to live abundantly before her life ends, in "The Day Is Fleet" it is only her desire for life's fullness that sustains this quest. Thus, the persona's demand, "Let the hours bloom triumphantly / Before life's little sun has set / And I am old," disguises an autonomy that rejects the very nature of the abrupt, swift-moving sun and day, while also ridiculing the sun's transformative power as "little." Again, Johnson uses her poetic persona to undermine hierarchies operating in the metaphorical daylight. The persona also connects the sun with aging, suggesting that decline and the premium placed on a youthful body exists in the sunlit, physical world. As this world would regard death as the natural process of inevitable decline accompanied by older age, the persona evokes this version of death to emphasize her attachment to the rejuvenating form of death in "Escape." Accordingly, when she declares, "The day is fleet / And I / Am far too passionate / To die!," she suggests that the passion emanating from her core self is time resistant and a shield from decline.

Johnson's reconceptualization of darkness and death frame the desire for freedom and erotic attachment as engendering components of Black female subjectivity. This centering of Black female interiority in opposition to metaphorical daylight demonstrates Johnson's modernist preoccupation with "artistic release of an inner voice unfettered by society's imprisoning restraints . . . and pursuing beautiful truth from within."[67] Her sensibility for redefining spaces to create transcendent moments of solace and lasting revelation also places her in conversation with Angelina Weld Grimké, Gwendolyn B. Bennett, and Mae V. Cowdery. As Maureen Honey argues, these three New Negro poets created "an Aphrodite figure who compels respect and casts off the fetters of racist patriarchal civilization, symbolized by her dark body's emergence after nightfall." Reigning in darkness, the conjured goddess who modeled a new kind of power in the modern age "inhabited a realm that released her speakers from false inhibiting roles played out during daytime routines."[68] Complete with flora and fauna, this realm's natural world created an inviting landscape set in opposition to the racism and patriarchal rule of urban spaces. Johnson's persona in *Tears* does not envision a dark-skinned goddess, but in the collection's third section, the persona shifts concentration from symbolic darkness to a transgressive reenvisioning of the natural world. While the majority of poems in the section titled "Nor This, nor That" attest to the complexities of biracial identity—a subject in line with integrationist sentiment present in some African American political organizations during the 1940s—particular poems employ nature imagery to evidence a direct challenge to patriarchal order. "World Contained" represents one such poem:

Behold—
A grappled son of men,
A fusion of their strength,
I overreach their breadth and girth
And overleap their length.

The whole world is my Amazon,
I pulse at every pore;
Armoured in jest I live full fierce
As no man lived before.

Here, the persona evokes a central tenet of this section: the biracial subject's capacity to claim as a matter of pride and salvific potential the combination of racial identities distilled in blood. On a deeper register, however, we find the undermining of traditional symbols denoting male authority by a persona who reinterprets these symbols in service to an empowered, Black female body. Indeed, the persona presents the Black female body as a supreme, corrected version of a male body, thus inverting traditional binaries that read deficiency in Black and female bodies. Identifying herself first as "A grappled son of men," the persona claims the sex of those who struggle. Yet the allusions to "breadth," "girth," and "length" suggest that the origin of this heritage of struggle lies in an unacknowledged anxiety relative not simply to penis size but to the arbitrary nature of using anatomy to declare governing authority. Nonetheless, the persona appears to accept this false determiner of power, declaring the ability to "overreach" and "overleap," thus restoring confidence in phallocentric social and political arrangements. However, true to Johnson's personal and creative investment in disrupting convention, the persona in the second stanza reveals that the descriptors, "breadth," "girth," and "length" signal the Amazon as ultimate authority. Connecting herself with the naturally vast, forceful, and pulsating Amazon rather than the contrived authority derived from male anatomy demonstrates the persona reclaiming female identity, but it also makes the South American river and forest representative of edifying truth again geographically and conceptually separated from urban spaces. The Amazon becomes a "revisionist metaphor," a term Alicia Ostriker employs to denote women writers' imaginative use of "the natural as opposed to the artificial" to commend the physical self.[69] Maintaining this transgressive orientation at the poem's conclusion, the persona suggests that portraying her physical self as male, then female, serves as a form of jest, a mode of disruption that provides cover for insightful critique that leads to living "full fierce" and uniquely free.

The poem's triumphant conclusion perhaps obscures another defiant reading operating at its beginning, one that implies a relationship between Christianity and patriarchy. That Johnson writes, "Behold," and then allows this declaration to occupy the poem's first line rehearses Christ's usage of this command and imbues it with deference symbolized by its solitary presence. That the reader is instructed to behold "A grappled son of men" not only repurposes Christ's designation of himself as "The Son of Man," but it reverses the perspective in John 19:27. Whereas this biblical account records Christ during his crucifixion instructing his mother and disciple to behold each other as mother and son, the first and second lines of the poem shift our view not to others but to a figure suggestive of Christ in struggle. Because the deconstruction of male power follows in the poem, the persona connects this power with a particular form of Christianity ostensibly focused on Christ but that actually distorts the very meaning of Christian sacrifice to validate unequal relations between men and women. Thus, Johnson indicates that in this crucial moment of sacrifice, Christ agonizes as a result of his crucifixion but further struggles because of misguided readings of Christian tenets. Through her persona, Johnson insists that distorted interpretations of Christianity symbolized by the poem's metaphorical suffering Christ affirm patriarchy rather than concentrating on Christ's actual message of mutual respect between men and women, an ideology he endorses when communicating with his mother and disciple.

This multivalent representation of Christianity finds complement in poems that evoke Christian imagery. "Perspective" celebrates the persona's commitment to redemptive suffering for "a race burgeoning," and it infuses the persona's pain with sacred significance that will eventually prompt her to "bless the thorns / That wound me!" Offering a conflicting, humanist sensibility, the reprinted and renamed poem "The Beggar Is a Fool" suggests the absurdity of prioritizing supplication over uncompromising determination that manifests in a commanding voice reflective of progressive, secular commitments.[70] In the collection's last two sections, however, Johnson's critical assessment no longer embraces or departs from Christian tenets, and she expands the meaning of personal liberation in redefined spaces to include collective redemption. She does this by transporting readers to the Garden of Eden, a location that doubles as an imaginative historical moment that predates Christianity—and therefore nullifies some sexists' religious justification for gender inequality—and a natural space wherein men attain spiritual sustenance from a world devoid of exclusionary ideology.

This investment in historical return illustrates Johnson's use of history as a rejoinder to supremacist practices, "a strategy with philosophical underpinnings" used by postbellum African American poets to "refute the essentialism of stereotypes and the pseudo-science on race."[71] That Johnson evokes this tradition in the sections "With Level Look" and "The Gulf of Challenge" reflects the stylistic features postbellum poets bequeathed to Harlem Renaissance writers but, more incisively, her manipulation of this convention to oppose and remake a world suffering from racism and sexism.

Johnson's adaptation of this strategy not only evidences the possibility of collective transcendence, but it also demonstrates that her modernist imagination has the capacity to shape history. Therefore, she elevates the postbellum Black subject's claim to humanity as a Black figure capable of "change over time" and adaptable to the demands of democracy and modernization by creating a restorative space that allows Black and white persons supporting prejudicial beliefs to return to the site of creation and work toward "change over time." Thus, Johnson reimagines the criteria for those requiring development by suggesting that those who preclude Black persons and women from actualizing personhood are ill suited for democratic participation.

Representing how such persons inform the body politic and the exclusionary, contradictory reality that necessitates an imaginative return to the Garden of Eden, Johnson first identifies an arrogant pride that disregards the lived experiences of those with curtailed power. She facilitates this critique while appearing only to champion an integrationist or pacifist message by questioning the implications of African Americans' participation in war. In fact, while the "brotherhood" message or theme that Johnson embraces later in life characterizes the majority of poems in the remaining two sections, her use of irony and interrogation in particular poems keep women's circumscribed identities and the necessity for redemption at the center of her incisive criticism. In "Negro Mother Prays," for example, Johnson's persona as Black mother reveals to God that her "deeply travailed" state arises from having sent her sons "across the sea" "To fight a fight for those whose hands / Are cords about their throats." She then evokes the State's denial of civil liberties, but she does so with questions and answers that interpret fighting as colluding in Black oppression, while ostensibly appealing to a higher power to demystify Black subjugation: "What are they fighting for? / Oh can it be for manhood-rights / Here in their native land, /

Or does it serve some other end I do not understand?" Maintaining this critical mode, the persona concludes the poem with pointed questions that image Black subservience as the consequences of patriotic service. Before petitioning God to intervene in this racist arrangement to prevent her "gallant sons" from "returning home / To live on bended knee," she wonders:

> Whose freedom is it, God, I ask,
> Demanding blood of me?
> Am I to look at this long last
> Upon real liberty?
>
> Or is it that my sons but fight
> That other men may be
> Reclining in a triumph-car
> That we draw heavily?

The persona's queries saturate the poem with irony, compelling readers to ponder not only deceptive, racist arrangements beneath the veneer of celebrated, national achievement but also the ways in which this critique clarifies other oppressive social structures. Therefore, the supremacist structure operating in the poem might also be read as ironic commentary on the sexist limitations that Black women confront within their own racial community. When the persona indicts war as a collective enterprise that actually conceals nefarious intentions, she also describes the creative and social strictures imposed on Black women to support a masculinist uplift strategy. Through her persona, then, Johnson suggests that the oppressive strategies Black women confronted during the 1920s remain in currency in the 1940s. While condemning the ideology of white supremacy, Johnson also rejects supremacist formations generally applied. Thus, "Negro Mother Prays" locates fault in white and Black men loyal to supremacism and suggests that these groups must enter a restorative space to divest themselves of this devotion.[72]

While "Black Recruit" reinforces the ironic tone in "Negro Mother Prays," "Question" argues that Black men's investment in gender hierarchy emasculates them, rendering them unprepared to challenge those descending "Into the whirling, maggot sands / Of prejudice."[73] Even when the persona in "In Your Treaty" considers an end to war and the drafting of a treaty, her request in the poem's final lines again exposes Black women's plight, but triumphantly assumes that God would also occupy their ostracized position: "Don't dismiss us with a nod, / Lest you mistake and leave us / On the outside there with God." In a transition from poetry descriptive of racial and gender exclusion, "This Hour" serves as the transition point between insider/outsider status and entrance into the transformative Garden. The persona proclaims:

> This is the hour of destiny,
> The scales of Time now sway;
> Shall we be gathered to the night,
> Or see a better day?

As she has previously designated night a rejuvenating space for women, the persona masks the restorative implications of darkness by interpreting this space as a metaphor for regressive action in opposition to envisioning "a better day." She also makes clear that the prospect of seeing "a better day," and thus existing in a world no longer invested in racism and sexism, is directly tied to the fluidity of time during this decisive hour. Emphasizing the weight and transportive nature of this moment, in "Brotherhood," she declares, "Come, Brothers, all!" then asks, "Shall we not wend / The blind way of our prison world." The men reach the garden in "Foregather," but instead of the persona describing the lush, fecund landscape, she chooses to detail the eventual effect of this environment on men's previous relation to power and anticipates a world remade. Johnson writes:

Nor white nor black shall habitate the earth,
But like a rainbow, men shall web and span
The turning globe. The eagle eye may scan
The mingled colours of its living girth—
None may assail the equity of birth.
False values vanish—this shall be the plan,
The mark, the count, the goal to any man
Who runs with courage on the course of earth.

And war shall lift its clutches from the land,
Men shall go forth like children hand in hand,
Vaunting the vision of the recent blind,
Rapt in the vista of the unchained mind.
They shall regather and again recall
The trail lost somewhere since the primal Fall.

If recollection of a prelapsarian vision can foster equality in the future, then the origin of this previously lost vision derives from their current location. Accordingly, the persona's reference to "The trail lost somewhere since the primal Fall" not only looks forward to a world restored but also reflects the environment they inhabit, an imaginative Eden devoid of prejudice. In a manner that characterizes action in this environment and offers strategy for reclaiming a lost world, the persona suggests that the transformative nature of this space relieves inherited notions of power. Therefore, her assertion, "Nor white nor black shall habitate the earth," demonstrates the anticipated erasure of hierarchical structures both in the garden and throughout the remainder of human history. Not only is the relinquishing of false values and the end of wars the result of such erasure, but by referencing the relationship between sightedness and liberated thought, the persona confirms another benefit that evokes a major trope in African American literature. However, as a result of this new orientation that will manifest in "a better day" and these men's "change over time," the persona also implicitly transitions women from a position of racial and gender subjugation to a reconceptualized world and future absent of these values. While appearing only to endorse interracial corporation, then, Johnson employs her Black, female imagination to remake men, symbolically reversing the myth of human creation by re-creating men from part of a woman. Not only does the apparent absence of women from the reimagined Eden underscore this point, but it reemphasizes the argument that only men require further development. Furthermore, if we apply to this poem's Eden Zora Neale Hurston's symbolic representation of oppressive masculinity as a venomous snake capable of destroying men and interpersonal intimacy, the persona offers the garden without this intrusion to ensure the survival of re-created men.[74]

In line with Ronald Primeau's assessment of Johnson's creative impulse, through her persona she fashions a world that does not exist to create an environment wherein men access core selves liberated from divisive ideologies.[75] That *Tears* culminates in the image of reconstitution speaks to the potential Johnson invests in men and woman to manifest in reality her vision of a restored world. Yet it also seems to highlight her own desire for reconsideration. In the collection's final poem, she extends her preoccupation with renewed existence to include herself in a manner that anticipates her literary recovery. In a fitting end to *Tears*, "Resolution" provides an image of resurrection made coherent when read as a description of Johnson shorn of performative obligation.[76] That Cedric Dover takes the title of his introduction from the first line of "Resolution" underscores the connection this poem articulates between persona and poet. After confessing that she is "Close to the unrelenting sod," the persona transitions from acknowledgement of her proximity to death to an image of total vivification:

> But now a surging, wild unrest
> Uproots the poppies from my breast,
> My soul awake, erect, anew,

I stand and face the star-swept blue,
And swear to make my dreams come true!

As we've seen, *Tears* evidences some of Johnson's dreams, and although this poem foreshadows her death in 1966, its delight in the animating core self who resists decline suggests that her poetry serves as autobiographical testament to her most fervent yearnings. Thus, even as she evokes her own death, she reiterates the dream of knowing a free self unburdened by temporality and social expectations. Throughout her literary career, Johnson realized the personal benefits and social disadvantages of this dream, of claiming an identity beyond post-Victorian gentility and having her complex relationship with convention and critique assessed in relation to her bold imagination. The recovery of *After a Thousand Tears* in our contemporary moment, then, grants us the opportunity to fulfill this dream and move toward a fuller appreciation of Johnson as artist and individual.

The volume that follows reproduces the original manuscript in the order in which it appeared among Dover's papers, save that the contents page has been removed, updated, and placed at the start of *this* book. The original volume placed many shorter poems on the same page, whereas for this volume, I have opted to place each poem on its own. The text follows that of the original typescript. That said, the original volume was typewritten, while this volume has been professionally typeset, meaning that as per convention, some standard changes have been made: for example, space around periods and in ellipses has been adjusted and standardized, British-style quote marks changed to American, spaced hyphens that stood in for dashes have been rendered as dashes, full-cap titles have been changed to headline style, underline has been rendered as italics, line spaces have been removed between paragraphs in the prose, and line endings have been adjusted to account for the change in trim size and font.

NOTES

1. *The Crisis*, January 1919, 111.

2. Nina Miller, *Making Love Modern: The Intimate Public Worlds of New York's Literary Women* (New York: Oxford University Press, 1999), 152.

3. Alain Locke, *The New Negro: An Interpretation* (New York: Albert and Charles Boni, 1925), ix.

4. Erin D. Chapman, *Prove It on Me: New Negroes, Sex, and Popular Culture in the 1920s* (New York: Oxford University Press, 2012), 77.

5. Maureen Honey, ed., *Shadowed Dreams: Women's Poetry of the Harlem Renaissance*, 2nd ed. (New Brunswick, N.J.: Rutgers University Press, 2006), xxxv.

6. Gloria T. Hull, *Color, Sex, and Poetry: Three Women Writers of the Harlem Renaissance* (Bloomington: Indiana University Press, 1987), 21. Erin D. Chapman uses the phrase "mother the race" to denote the expectation for Black women to "devote themselves to the maintenance and welfare of the greater black family, gladly serving everyone except themselves." Chapman concludes that this gender discourse muted Black women's voices and "did little to eliminate the particular oppression that continued to assault them." Chapman, *Prove It on Me*, 77.

7. In a letter dated December 26, 1944, Johnson writes, "Sent away two books yesterday. After A Thousand Tears and Brotherhood. Am copying two others and two chapters of the Biography." GDJ to Jackman, December 26, 1944, box 19, folder 20, Countee Cullen–Harold Jackman Memorial Collection, Atlanta University Center Robert W. Woodruff Library.

8. While Johnson's relationship with Padma Publications remains unclear, she may have become familiar with the press through her friendship with the original author of the introduction to *Tears*, Anglo-Indian writer and race theorist Cedric Dover. Ostensibly typed by an editor at Padma, one sentence inside the front cover of *Tears* reveals, "*After a Thousand Tears* is prefaced with a critical evaluation by Cedric Dover, the well known Indian writer, whose name is so familiar to readers of Padma books." Johnson's investment in connecting people of different nationalities (most clearly visible in her creation of "One World: Washington Social Letter Club, Inc.," a correspondence club she ran during the 1940s) may also explain her interest in publishing with Padma. Furthermore, I suspect that because of Johnson's financial difficulties following her husband's death in 1925, she was not as selective with her choice of publishers, as she hoped monies earned from the sale of her publications would supplement her income.

9. Johnson's other volumes of poetry include *The Heart of a Woman And Other Poems* (1918), *Bronze: A Book of Verse* (1922), *An Autumn Love Cycle* (1928), and *Share My World* (1962).

10. Rejoicing in the implications of India's independence and African Americans' recognition of these implications relative to their own liberation struggle, Dover would later write, "I saw the whole Negro people share [India's] jubilation in 1947." Qtd. in Nico Slate, *The Prism of Race: W. E. B. Du Bois, Langston Hughes, Paul Robeson, and the Colored World of Cedric Dover* (New York: Palgrave Macmillan, 2014), 21.

11. Qtd. in Hull, *Color, Sex, and Poetry*, 210.

12. Claudia Tate, *Selected Works of Georgia Douglas Johnson* (Boston: G. K. Hall & Co., 1997), xxxix, qtd. in Winona Fletcher, "Georgia Douglas Johnson," *Dictionary of Literary Biography*, vol. 51, *Afro-American Writers from the Harlem Renaissance to 1940*, ed. Trudier Harris and Thadious M. Davis (Detroit: Gale Group, 1987), 163.

13. In *The Plays of Georgia Douglas Johnson*, Judith L. Stephens presents the first book to focus on Johnson as playwright, and she includes all of Johnson's extant plays in the volume. Judith L. Stephens, *The Plays of Georgia Douglas Johnson: From The New Negro Renaissance to the Civil Rights Movement* (Champaign: University of Illinois Press, 2006): 3.

14. Tate, *Selected Works of Georgia Douglas Johnson*, xxxvii.

15. In a letter written to Jackman on August 8, 1944, Johnson confides, "Have about eight books here ready to get going—three new books of poetry, thirty plays both one and three act, thirty short stories, a novel, a book of philosophy, a book of exquisite sayings . . . twenty songs. . . . [S]eems I must go to that last peaceful abode without getting them printed . . . but why should I be worrying. Balzac left forty unpublished books." Three years later Johnson informs Dover that she has thirty unpublished books, to which Dover responds, "Anyone who has written 30 unpublished books has been pouring out words for years, without much thought for selectiveness, audience, and the making of publishable books." Dover cautions Johnson to "write nothing more until you have thoroughly sifted and weeded out all this material and reduced it to manageable proportions." Dover to GDJ, July 16, 1947, box 1, folder 27, Georgia Douglas Johnson Papers at Howard University's Moorland-Spingarn Research Center, Washington, D.C., qtd. in Hull, *Color, Sex, and Poetry*, 189.

16. Johnson published "Gesture" (1936) and "Tramp Love" (1937) using

the pseudonym Paul Tremaine. She also wrote syndicated columns in the 1940s and 1950s under the alias Mary V. Strong. Johnson would also publish "Beauty Hints by Nina Temple." Claudia Tate suspects that Johnson's "acquisition of a post office box—P.O Box 6345, Washington 9, D.C.—was to facilitate her correspondence in a variety of names and the management of her correspondence club under the name M. Strong." Johnson also used aliases M. Strong, John Tremaine, John Temple, Ninevah Gladstone, Miriam Nosra, Lorraine Lillith, and Bessie Brent Wilson. Tate, *Selected Works of Georgia Douglas Johnson*, lxxii–lxxiii

17. Qtd. in Hull, *Color, Sex, and Poetry*, 202.

18. In 1938, Johnson admits, "You see Paul Tremain is one of my pseudonyms. I used it on the stories. I rewrote them you know and feel kind of a pride in their reception. I only changed the form of expression etc. not the content." GDJ to Jackman, August 4, 1938, box 19, folder 20, Countee Cullen–Harold Jackman Memorial Collection.

19. Tate, *Selected Works of Georgia Douglas Johnson*, xxxiii.

20. See Erlene Stetson's "Rediscovering the Harlem Renaissance: Georgia Douglas Johnson, 'The New Negro Poet.'" *Obsidian* 5, no. 1/2 (1979): 28.

21. Johnson's mother, Laura (née Douglas), was Black and Native American. Her father, George Camp, was Black and white.

22. Johnson, qtd. in "The Contest Spotlight," *Opportunity*, July 1927, 204.

23. In *Making Love Modern*, Nina Miller evidences the implications for speaking selves in women's poetry that draws on the "lyric moment." Miller, *Making Love Modern*, 211.

24. Countee Cullen, ed., *Caroling Dusk: An Anthology of Verse by Negro Poets* (New York: Harper, 1927), 74.

25. Although she traveled extensively in the latter half of the 1920s, Johnson would live the remainder of her life in Washington, D.C.

26. Mark A. Sanders, "Toward a Modernist Poetics," in *The Cambridge History of African American Literature*, ed. Maryemma Graham and Jerry W. Ward Jr. (Cambridge, UK: Cambridge University Press, 2015), 221.

27. Ibid. This collective supremacist vision by white Americans in the North and South helped to restore a sense of national unity in the years following the Civil War.

28. James Weldon Johnson echoes this sentiment, writing in his 1922 "Preface" to *The Book of American Negro Poetry*, "No people that has pro-

duced great literature and art has ever been looked upon by the world as distinctly inferior." James Weldon Johnson, "Preface," in *The Book of American Negro Poetry* (New York: Harcourt Brace, 1922), vii.

29. Ajuan Maria Mance, *Inventing Black Women: African American Women Poets and Self-Representation, 1877–2000* (Knoxville: University of Tennessee Press, 2007), 56.

30. In *The Sexual Mountain and Black Women Writers*, Calvin Hernton frames this dynamic: "Historically the battle line of the racial struggle in the United States has been drawn exclusively as a struggle between the men of the races. Everything having to do with race has been defined and counter-defined by men as a question of whether black people were or were not a race of Men. The central concept and the universal metaphor around which all aspects of the racial situation revolve is 'Manhood.' Whatever whites have done to blacks, it is viewed, by the men, not as the wrongdoing on an entire people, males and females. Rather, it is viewed solely in terms of the denial of the MANHOOD of a people." Calvin Hernton, *The Sexual Mountain and Black Women Writers: Adventures in Sex, Literature, and Real Life* (Anchor Books, 1990), 38.

31. Mance, *Inventing Black Women*, 57.

32. See Miller, *Making Love Modern*, 153.

33. Elise Johnson McDougald, "The Task of Negro Womanhood," in Locke, *New Negro*, 382.

34. Chapman argues that in this marketplace "New Negroes consumed versions of their own ideologies and subjectivities, many of them shaped by or against race motherhood." Chapman, *Prove It on Me*, 77.

35. W. E. B. Du Bois, "The Criteria of Negro Art," *The Crisis*, October 1926.

36. Martin Summers, *Manliness and Its Discontents: The Black Middle Class and the Transformation of Masculinity, 1990–1930* (Chapel Hill: University of North Carolina Press, 2004), 202.

37. Locke, *New Negro*, 15.

38. Such praise helped earn her the distinction "The foremost woman poet of the race." This phrase, attributed to William Stanley Braithwaite, was often used in reference to Johnson.

39. Qtd. in Hull, *Color, Sex, and Poetry*, 180.

40. Tate, *Selected Works of Georgia Douglas Johnson*, lviii.

41. Foreword to *Bronze: A Book of Verse* (Boston: B. J. Brimmer Co.,

1922), 7; Du Bois, Georgia Douglas Johnson Recommendation, November 16, 1927, W. E. B Du Bois Papers (MS 312), Special Collections and University Archives, University of Massachusetts Amherst Libraries.

42. See Marita Bonner, "On Being Young—a Woman—and Colored," *The Crisis*, December 1925.

43. In a diary entry dated October 1, 1921, Alice Dunbar-Nelson remembers that while visiting Johnson's home, Henry Lincoln Johnson was especially interested in her teaching Johnson "how to put on hats." Claudia Tate maintains that "if knowing 'how to put on hats' was publicly sanctioned feminine knowledge, the mature Johnson learned her lessen well. She was seldom seen in public without a hat, as her numerous photographs reveal." Tate, *Selected Works of Georgia Douglas Johnson*, xliii.

44. As evidenced in *Forgotten Readers*, Saturday night visitors included Jean Toomer, Langston Hughes, Countee Cullen, Jessie Fauset, Wallace Thurman, William Stanley Braithwaite, Charles S. Johnson, Zora Neale Hurston, Arna Bontemps, Alain Locke, Kelly Miller, James Weldon Johnson, W. E. B. Du Bois, Alice Dunbar-Nelson, Mary "Mamie" Burrill, Gwendolyn Bennett, Chandler Owen, Willis Richardson, Lewis Alexander, Marita Boner, Mollie Gibson Brewer, Grant Lucas, Angelina Weld Grimké, Effie Lee Newsome, Richard Bruce Nugent, Montgomery Gregory, Rebecca West, Anne Spencer, Wright Cuney, E. C. Williams, B. K. Bruce, Glenn Carrington, Mae Miller, Adella Parks, Frank Horne, and Mae Howard Jackson. Elizabeth McHenry, *Forgotten Readers: Recovering the Lost History of African American Literary Societies* (Durham: Duke University Press, 2002), 274, 287.

45. McHenry, *Forgotten Readers*, 268; Langston Hughes, *The Big Sea: An Autobiography* (New York: Hill and Wang, 2002), 216. Relative to her importance to the Harlem Renaissance and its writers, Glenn Carrington writes in his memoir, "If Dr. Alain Locke was godfather to the younger writers and artists, Mrs. Johnson was certainly their godmother." Glenn Carrington, "The Harlem Renaissance: A Personal Memoir," *Freedomways* 3, no. 3 (Summer 1963): 309

46. Qtd in Hull, *Color, Sex, and Poetry*, 179.

47. The gay and lesbian writers with whom Johnson communicated include Alain Locke, Langston Hughes, Glenn Carrington, Mary Burrill, Angelina Weld Grimké, Bruce Nugent, Wallace Thurman, and Harold Jackman. Johnson was closest to Carrington and Jackman.

48. Du Bois to Johnson, [illegible] 17, 1926, box 162, folder 29, GDJ Papers.

49. Dunbar-Nelson writes, "You might call it poetic inspiration, if you will, but it looks suspiciously to me as if Georgia had an affair, and it had been a source of inspiration to her." Alice Dunbar-Nelson, *Give Us Each Day: The Diary of Alice Dunbar-Nelson*, ed. Gloria T. Hull (New York: W. W. Norton, 1984), 88.

50. Foreword to Georgia Douglas Johnson, *An Autumn Love Cycle* (New York: Harold Vinal, Limited; Binghampton, New York: Vali-Ballou Press, 1928), xviii. The pseudonymous description was written under the name Michael Victor Strong. Strong provides this description in the preface to *Share My World*.

51. Georgia Douglas Johnson, *The Heart of a Woman and Other Poems* (Boston: Cornhill Company, 1918), 1.

52. Honey, *Shadowed Dreams*, xlvii.

53. Qtd. in Hull, *Color, Sex, and Poetry*, 179.

54. Keith D. Leonard, "African American Women Poets and the Power of the Word," in *The Cambridge Companion to African American Women's Literature*, ed. Angelyn Mitchell and Danille K. Taylor (Cambridge, UK: Cambridge University Press, 2009), 173.

55. Ibid., 169. See also Hazel Carby, *Reconstructing Womanhood: The Emergence of the Afro-American Woman Novelist* (New York: Oxford University Press, 1987), 6.

56. Hull, *Color, Sex, and Poetry*, 177.

57. Introduction to Johnson, *Heart of a Woman*, vii.

58. Cedric Dover, "One Life Full Certified," this volume.

59. Ibid.

60. Slate, *Prism of Race*, 11.

61. Dover, "One Life Full Certified."

62. Ralph Ellison, "Richard Wright's Blues," *Antioch Review* 5, no. 2 (1945): 62.

63. Audre Lorde, *A Burst of Light and Other Essays* (Mineola, N.Y.: Ixia Press, 2017), 130.

64. Cheryl Wall, *Women of the Harlem Renaissance* (Bloomington: Indiana University Press, 1995), 14–15.

65. Johnson expresses a similar, ironic orientation in the poem "Ivy."

66. These lines are from the poem "One Lives Too Long." The sensibility

reflected here takes a romantic notion of death (for example, Keats's speaker in "Ode to a Nightingale" who reveals, "I have been half in love with easeful Death, / Call'd him soft names in many a mused rhyme, / Now more than ever seems it rich to die") and repurposes it to express an aspect of Black women's experience.

67. Maureen Honey, *Aphrodite's Daughters: Three Modernist Poets of the Harlem Renaissance* (New Brunswick, N.J.: Rutgers University Press, 2016): 10.

68. Ibid., 8.

69. Alicia Ostriker, *Stealing the Language: The Emergence of Women's Poetry in America* (Boston: Beacon Press, 1986), 108.

70. With minor revisions in this volume, "Perspective" was previously published in *Bronze*. "The Beggar Is a Fool" is a slightly revised, renamed version of "The Suppliant," also previously published in *Bronze*.

71. Sanders, "Toward a Modernist Poetics," 224.

72. As Judith L. Stephens highlights in her introduction to *The Plays of Georgia Douglas Johnson*, Johnson's investment in concentrating attention on supremacist values and their manifestation led her to compose numerous lynching dramas. She remains the most prolific playwright of the lynching drama tradition.

73. With minor revisions in this volume, "Question" was previously published in *Bronze*.

74. I refer here to Hurston's short story "Sweat" (1926) and her parallel of Sykes with the snake he uses to terrify his wife, Delia.

75. Ronald Primeau, "The Renaissance Re-examined," in *The Harlem Renaissance Remembered*, ed. Arna Bontemps (New York: Dodd, Mead & Co., 1972), 266.

76. With revisions in this volume, "Resolution" was previously published in *Bronze* and *Share My World*.

AFTER
A THOUSAND TEARS

By

GEORGIA DOUGLAS JOHNSON

WITH AN INTRODUCTION BY CEDRIC DOVER

A PADMA PUBLICATION   Rs 0/0

Mrs. Georgia Douglas Johnson is a distinguished Negro American, whose sensitive lyrics and fighting poems have warmed the hearts of her people for over three decades. She has published several books, and her work is represented in all the anthologies of Negro poetry, but this selection of her poems is the first to be published in India. It reveals her personal landscape, her responses to the Aframerican scene, and her deep feeling for "the something we call human."

It is a distillation, in fact, of a rich personality, typical of liberal thought throughout the coloured world. Therefore it is an essential book, made more valuable by its sincere and direct simplicity, for those who want to know the feelings and attitudes of the rising coloured peoples. For India it has a most intimate interest.

After a Thousand Tears is prefaced with a critical evaluation by Cedric Dover, the well-known Indian writer, whose name is so familiar to readers of Padma books.

For

THOSE WHO WOULD UNDERSTAND

These bits of verse sound here and there along the scale of Tolerance, as the heart meditates or cries aloud when certain notes are touched.

And because they sound the heartbeat at the moment of contact, they might strike a chord that leads to better understanding.

Georgia Douglas Johnson

ONE LIFE FULL CERTIFIED

Cedric Dover

It is said, with just enough exaggeration to point the truth, that the Negroes are behind everything creative in the United States. They have not only made the outstanding folk culture of colonised America, but have a remarkable gift for absorbing and transforming which goes beyond imitation to the making of novelties that are more than merely clever. This characteristic gave life to the artistic upsurge known as the New Negro Movement. Its vitality, expertly distilled by Alain Locke in *The New Negro* and V. F. Calverton in his *Anthology of American Negro Literature*, is as urban as the blues and as notable as any achievement during the effulgence of the 'twenties.

Georgia Douglas Johnson's poems have been published in the anthologies of this "renaissance," her three books appeared in the decade that marked its beginning and end, and her home has always been a centre for the writers and artists who gave it colour and shape. She is definitely of it; but equally definitely not in it. Her first volume, *The Heart of a Woman* (1918), echoes Sara Teasdale and shows a fine sensibility, but contains no hint of the ferment which, a little later, inspired Claude McKay's moving sonnets of protest, his evocative explorations of the Harlem scene, and his exquisite lyrics of nostalgia.

Claude McKay's *Harlem Shadows* heralded the paganism which was to grow into the glorification of the Golden Brown and the portrayal of the sordid realities of city life. These extensions of poetic function required freedom from the restraints of conventional poetising, and found it in the work of Carl Sandburg, Vachel Lindsay and other figures of the American "poetry revival." There was no lack of new forms for expressing new values.

Bronze (1922), Mrs. Johnson's second book, reflects these departures from the vision of the comfortable villa in the manner indicated by its title. The subject is still the heart of a woman, but now it is the heart of a coloured woman aware of her social problem and the potentiality of the hybrid. Unfortunately her last book, *An Autumn Love Cycle* (1928), fails to concentrate her awareness. Instead of enlarging the new vitality, it reverts to the personal notes of her first, with the aching maturity of a sensitive woman in her forties. In it the poet is again overcome by herself.

Soon after the *Cycle*, the Depression swept away the Golden Brown and everything else that was supposedly golden in the days of mad prosperity. It should, by all analogies, have swept Mrs. Johnson away too, but she survived by turning her attention to other things, including fiction. The war revived her into fighting identification with the Negro struggle to share the democracy that demanded Negro lives and labour. She gave herself unstintingly and, at the same time, poured out a stream of effective poems and martial songs. Today, in her early sixties, she remains as vital as she was thirty years ago.

It is an exceptional record. All the more exceptional when we view the sad procession of middle class poets silenced by inability to find some dynamic in a transitional society. Mrs. Johnson has been saved, I think, from this fate by the circumstance of being a Negro. It has prevented class limitations from enclosing, and finally stifling, her. It rouses a passionate belief, grounded in suffering, in ultimate justice and the coming brotherhood of man. It gives that extra something, supported by keen poetic sense, apparent in her great sincerity and appealing simplicity.

These are qualities that assure admiration, even from those who have gone beyond idealisation to the real means, the critical disciplines and endeavor, by which ideals are realised. They are evident in the sifting of her collected work presented here for the first time. It is lit by the glow of a rich, mellow personality, near enough to less generously endowed folk to be typical of cultivated thought in a large part of the coloured world.

Indeed her affinities with people and poetry we know are as integral to the interest of her poems as the quietly sharp difference. We expect chords of conventional familiarity among the offerings in "The Heart of a Woman," and we find them—yet their essential quality is hedonistic. They do not chant the hymnals of undying devotion, but frankly sing the pleasures of loving today and sorrowing, if needs be, tomorrow. Again, in "Ambergris to Gall," the usual regrets of the passing years do not fuse, as they normally do, into uniform greyness, but suggest a personal adjustment based on the continued joy of being alive.

These two sections represent the chief preoccupations of ordinary feminine poesy. Mrs. Johnson escapes their fatal attractions through additional areas of awareness created by identification with Negro life. She has faced and resolved the psychological and social complications of being a near-white in the coloured scene, while retaining enough traces of "tragic octoroon" feeling to stress the merit of her conquest. She has felt this situation so intimately, and approached it with such courage, persistence and intuitive understanding, that she is still the first and most prolific poet of the half-caste, though Langston Hughes and the Eurasian, George Walker, have also probed the subject.

And it is from this distinction, not exhaustively indicated in "Not This, Nor That," that her community with the Aframerican people and her conspicuous urge to internationalism proceeds. There is a lesson here for those who would understand the social role of the mixed breed, as well as for the millions of mixed breeds themselves who are now caught up by vast changes in the balance of power and ideas—a lesson of basic importance. That is why I am especially proud of the opportunity to pay this tribute to my friend Georgia Douglas Johnson.

I. THE HEART OF A WOMAN

SOMETHING

Something for each of us
Surely somewhere,
Something the soul needs
Infinitely there.
Press through the dark
The gloom and the rain,
Life holds a balm
For each ravishing pain.
Something for each of us:
Do not despair,
There's a heart to yours answering
Fully—somewhere.

AND NOTHING MISS

Hold moments freighted sweet with joy
Supreme, distil with care
Their essence, let no frontier bar
A full fruition, fortune fair
Smiles once, and then speeds lightly on,
Nor can the fleetest thought retake
The lissom phantom, nor remake
One golden hour; afteryears
Are full enough of turgid tears.
Then fill the fragile cup of bliss
To brimming, drink!—and nothing miss!

PILGRIMAGE

Lend me a candle by whose light
I may discern the road
That winds into that magic path
Which leads to Love's abode.

THE MEASURE

Fierce is the conflict—the battle of eyes,
Sure and unerring, the wordless replies,
Challenges flash from their ambushing caves—
Men, by their glances, are masters or slaves.

QUERY

Is she the sage who will not sip
The cup love presses to her lip?
Or she who drinks the mad cup dry,
And turns with smiling face—to die?

CELIBACY

Where is the love that might have been
Flung to the four far ends of earth?
In my body stamping around,
In my body like a hound,
Leashed and restless—
Biding time!

PAST SPLENDOUR

My dear
The world would say
That you had tricked me
Wantonly—usurped my soul,
Then cast to dust my broken frame.
But ah!
It does not know
The priceless treasure of your sway.
The glory of a dynasty
Now passed away!

PARADOX

I know you love me better cold,
Strange as the pyramids of old,
Responselessly.
But I am frail, and spent, and weak
With surging torrents that bespeak
A living fire.
So, like a veil, my poor disguise
Is draped to save me from your eyes'
Deep challenges.
Fain would I fling this robe aside
And from you, in your bosom hide
Eternally.
Alas! you love me better cold,
Like frozen pyramids of old,
Unyieldingly?

BUT NOW . . . .

I shall be lonely in my grave
Where willows cast their slender shade
Above me. But now I crave
Response for which my heart was made.

My heart shall cease to sing some day
But now I want to leap and dance
And in some wild wood lose my way
And leave my destiny to chance.

WHILE YOU LOVE ME

I want to die while you love me,
While yet you held me fair,
While laughter lies upon my lips
And lights are in my hair.

I want to die while you love me,
And I bear to that still bed
Your kisses, turbulent, unspent,
To warm me when I'm dead.

I want to die while you love me—
Oh who would care to love
Till love has nothing more to ask
And nothing more to give?

EMPTINESS

All of the petty baubles spread
Are not the answers to my need,
These tinselled trappings but beguile
This journeying, while deep within
An urge unspeakable resides
That calls and calls unceasingly—
So hungering. No banquet spread
Can tempt it, and no golden wine
Make it forget: I balance it,
The world flies upward in the scale!
And yet, unsoothed, unquieted,
It calls and calls across the days,
Across the nights that sum my life.

REMEMBER

When Love's brief dream is done
Pass on. Nor hope to see again
The burnished glow of yesterday
Gone with its setting sun.

Know this, the little while of love
Is fleeting as a cloud,
As lissom as a zephyr's breath,
As fickle as a crowd.

Its gleaming rainbow flames the sky—
Enthralls—then fades from sight:
Love for a day, an hour and then—
Remember through the night.

IVY

I am a woman,
Which means
I am insufficient.
I need
Something to hold me
Or perhaps uphold—
I am a woman.

TOY

You deck my body lavishly,
I'm sleek and overfed;
And yet my soul is perishing,
Denied of daily bread.

You make a plaything of my life,
My every trust betray;
And when I would be penitent,
You kiss my prayers away.

I LIVED IN HELL

I lived in hell the other day,
The red fires swept me fiendishly;
But now—the horrors fall and fade
Like ghosts that memory has made.

I lived in hell, even today—
(How swift the hot flames die away)
Submerged with kisses, I forget
The tears upon my pillow yet!

WE STAND MUTE

No words can paint such fragile imagery,
Those prismic gossamers that roll
Beyond the skyline of the soul—
We stand mute!

THE DAY IS FLEET

Let the hours bloom triumphantly
Before life's little sun has set
And I am old.

The day is fleet
And I
Am far too passionate
To die!

NO TOKENS

You said, "I'll send you roses till we meet!"
But I, mistrustful of the fitful flame
Love lifted, felt it were too small a claim
Upon you, so declined your fine conceit
Lest they, perchance, like mocking envoys came
To breathe a message poisonously sweet.
I bade you lay no token at my feet
Save love alone, that failing, who can blame?

I hold no trophy in my cloistered close
But memories more potent than a rose.
Their fairy curtains round about me fall
In answer to my heart's low whispered call;
You were my sun, I but a paling star,
You are my light no matter where you are!

AUTUMN

Believe me—when I say
That love like yours, at this belated hour,
Overwhelms me,
Stills the fount of thought!
I move as one newborn
And strange to swift transitions,
As from my prison door
I gaze
Into the blinding sunlight!

THE ONLY CURE

Cure one love with another
To cauterize the pain;
And when the old love surges,
Escape through love again.

To die is to remember,
To live is to forget;
So cool the old love embers
With new love, and forget.

TRIUNE

Life, love and death
My all!
The circuit of my sum:
The first, prerequisite,
The last, too sure—
With love, the fulcrum measuring
My span of human joy!

II. AMBERGRIS TO GALL

THE YEARS ROLL BY

The years roll by—
I cannot hold them even though I would;
I kiss my fingers to them with no sigh,
Even though I should perhaps
Cling to some tear-sweet moments
Ere they fly.
For I am being stripped of Time
And I must die.

ALL THINGS PASS

All things pass,
Nothing abides
Forever.
The sorrow and distress today
Shall disappear and pass away.
Nothing—not even happiness—
Is constant,
Nor kiss nor sigh nor fond caress
Shall know tomorrow's loveliness.

Yes,
All things pass
Like shadows in a looking glass;
And nothing in this world shall stay
Save memory,
Which shall remain
And whisper to the heart again.

HOKKU

I

I look into my glass—
Who is this woman old and grey
With lips so pale, I pray?

II

Old now, and grey,
I walk the cold uncaring streets . . .
None look my way!

III

O come prince charming!
The sun dips in the western sea . . .
White strands in my hair.

IV

O where hides my love?
The day fades to evening . . .
My heart grows cold.

V

A kiss? No, not one . . .
I fear a furnace to awake
And then the after cold!

VI

Love is an ancient art,
Yet love does not grow old.
It's born, it blooms, it goes.

VII

For refuge, I might marry you,
But 'twould be treason to my heart.
It would be lonely.

ONE LIVES TOO LONG

One lives too long:
The days grow pale
And never-ending grow the nights—
One lives too long.

Once, how I laughed and lightly cried
I'd live forever if I could;
But now I know the gift of death
Is merciful—when understood.

Within my vaulted heart
No echo lives of life's old song.
Just softly sandalled vanished feet . . .
One lives too long!

HEARTBREAK AGE

There's a time in the heart of a woman
When she comes to the end of the road,
When life has hushed its joyous song
And hope is a heavy load.

It's the time when none still deem her fair,
Nor smile to have her near;
A time when memories alone
Survive the falling tear.

Oh, this is the time a woman fears
When she enters the lone last stage;
To man it's just the close of life,
To women—it's Heartbreak Age.

MY GOWN

I'm going now a-marketing
To buy myself a gown;
Shall it be white, shall it be blue,
Shall it be red or brown?

Shall it be blue to match my eyes,
Or like my lips so red,
Or, like the autumn in my heart,
A sober brown instead?

And yet, and yet, hope dies so hard
And lifts a mocking light;
Oh shall I trust that feeble gleam
And make my new gown white?

I TIED MY HEART WITH STRING

To keep my heart from breaking
I tied it with a string
Woven of bits of everything
That caused my heart to sing;

That placed a smile upon my lips
And set my heart aglow
Repainting rainbows in my skies
As in the long ago.

I look into the darkened years
With trepidance and doubt;
Alas, alas what shall I do
When all my string gives out!

DISPOSSESSED

Day by day
The pristine glory of my frame
Declines.—
Life's lurid flame devours me.

Helplessly
I view the wreckage
In its wake;
Tomorrow . . . hide me
I would weep.

No more the triumvirate
Youth, wit and beauty win,
No more the noonday's saucy coup.

Faint lights and few
My portion—
And twilight kindliness!

DEAD DAYS

Dead days of rapture and despair
I would your hours exhume;
Renew their wildness once again,
Their rigour and perfume.

This calm cold desert, passion spent,
Pervades me like a pall;
Oh! for that red, red chromatique
From ambergris to gall!

STORE

Tomorrow!
As a mocking skull,
Come if you will.
Today was mine,
And in its shine
I did distil
Full mead of joy—
All fadeless, pure,
Through life's bleak changes to endure;
And, as I tread the dim-lit way
Festooned by sorrow,
I'll bear the smile of yesterday
Into tomorrow!

WISHES

I'm tired of pacing the pretty round
Of the ring of the thing I know;
I want to stand on the daylight's edge
And see where the sunsets go.

I want to sail on a swallow's tail
And look through the sky's blue grass;
I want to see if the dreams in me
Shall perish or come to pass.

I want to look through the moon's pale crook
And gaze on the moon man's face;
I want to keep all the tears I weep
And sail to some unknown place.

AT DUSK

At dusk how wearily I creep
Into the crescent arms of sleep;
How hushed and desolate the sky
As heartache croons a lullaby!

A SONG

She sang....

Surrendered years came trooping through my heart,
Freighted with tears and laughter, joy and pain;
I stood at April, starry-eyed, and then—
Ran down the gamut of my life again!

ESCAPE

Shadows, shadows,
Hug me round
So that I shall not be found
By sorrow.
She pursues me
Everywhere,
I can't lose her
Anywhere.
Fold me in your black
Abyss,
She will never
Look in this.
Shadows, shadows,
Hug me round
In your solitude
Profound.

TO AGE

You had your day—
Why envy Youth the joyous passing span
Of dewy morning that comes once,
Just once, to any man?

Too well you know
The afterwhile of sun and afternoon,
When grim realities awake
And break the heart, so soon.

WE WERE NOT MADE TO LIVE ALONE

We were not made to live alone,
To have no bosom near,
No one to feel as one withal,
No loved one close and dear.

We were not made to live alone—
All hours smart with pain,
When breaking hearts are calling,
Calling, seeking all in vain.

We were not made to live alone,
For comradeship we cry;
Oh wherefore should we live alone
When all alone we die?

III. NOR THIS, NOR THAT

NOR THIS, NOR THAT

Not wholly this nor that,
But wrought
Of alien bloods am I,
A product of the interplay
Of travelled hearts.
Estranged, yet not estranged, I stand
All comprehending;
From my estate
I view earth's frail dilemma;
Scion of fused strength am I,
All understanding,
Nor this, nor that,
Contains me.

WORLD CONTAINED

Behold—
A grappled son of men,
A fusion of their strength,
I overreach their breadth and girth
And overleap their length.

The whole world is my Amazon,
I pulse at every pore;
Armoured in jest I live full fierce
As no man lived before.

THE ULTIMATE MAN

I am the ultimate man—
Uniting into one
The many variants of earth
Strayed since the world began.

I am finality,
Combined humanity
Returning on the long lost trail . . .
At the hour of setting sun!

INTERBRED

I am the sum of many lands
Within my heart, within my hands
The tributary forces flow
In one tremendous undertow.

No puny measure times the beat
Of my precursal, charging feet.
All essences resolve in me
Like rivers rushing to the sea!

PERSPECTIVE

Someday—
I shall be glad that it was mine to be
A dark fore-runner of a race burgeoning;
I then shall know
The secret of life's calvary,
And bless the thorns
That wound me!

TOMORROW'S SUN SHALL SHINE

No, no, I live in no half-world,
Nor do I feel deprived;
The earth and all its bloods are mine.
So channelled, I've arrived
Where no one-blooded man could ever
Hope or strive to be;
For I am readied, made for life!
And life was made for me!

Pity me not, nor succour me
With platitudes and prayers;
I have but only struck my stride
Along life's thoroughfares.
Within my body bloods of earth
Assemble and combine;
For me tomorrow's fervid sun
Shall dawn, shall rise, shall shine!

THE RIDDLE

White men's children spread over the earth,
Like a rainbow of peace to the drawn-swords of birth;
Uniting the races, soft tinted to one,
The world-man, Cosmopolite, Everyman's son;
Whose blood is the sum of the red and the blue
With deep comprehension transcending the two—
Unriddle this riddle of outside-in,
White men's children in black men's skin.

I LAUGH AT THE WORLD

I laugh at the world:
That drop of black they so revile
Is heritage supreme;
It is the leaven of the whole,
The attar to redeem.
If I were fair and frail and gold,
Without that touch of sun,
I would be less than nothingness—
No rock to build upon!
And so I laugh,
Laugh at the world
Agaze with sneering lip;
For I am rich with secret lore
In which my roots may dip!

MIXED BLOOD

My blood cries out "unfetter me,"
For I would rise, I would be free;
Remove the tethers from my feet,
For I have wings, longtipped and fleet.

My fathers, brothers, sisters, all
Unhand me, muffled though I call;
Then look you deep into my eyes,
Unflinching and unglazed by lies.

Why did you fashion me I pray?
Just for a toy to fling away
Into the flotsam heap where hate
Stands barring every earthly gate?

MATERNAL REFLECTIONS

Proud?
Perhaps—and yet
I cannot say with surety
That I am happy thus to be
Responsible for this young life's embarking.
Is he not thrall to prevalent conditions?
Does not the day loom dark apace
To weave its cordon of disgrace
Around his lifted throat?
Is not this mezzotint enough and surfeit
For such prescience?
Ah, did I dare
Recall the pulsing life I gave,
And fold him in the kindly grave!

Proud?
Yes—yet hesitant and half-afraid
I view this child of sorrow!

THE BEGGAR IS A FOOL

Long have I beat with timid hands
    upon your leaden door,
Praying the patient, futile prayer
    my father prayed before
Now soft o'er the threshold
    there comes this counsel cool:
The strong demand, contend, prevail—
    the beggar is a fool!

THE SNARL

Too late to roll the tangled skein!
The knot is taut, the might have been

Passed with the pangs of yesterday
Whose secrets are revealed today.

Threads of remotest hues combine—
Can you unravel yours from mine?

World motifs are not thus undone
Like prowess might command the sun.

It's futile now and passing late
To disentwine the threads of Fate.

FUSION

How deftly does the gardener blend
This rose and that
To bud a new creation
More gorgeous and more beautiful
Than any parent portion;
And so
I trace within my warring blood
The tributary sources
That potently commingle
And sweep
With newborn forces!

IV. WITH LEVEL LOOK

SORROW SINGERS

Hear their viol-voices ringing
Down the corridor of years,
As they lift their twilight faces
Through a mist of falling tears!

I GAZE INTO THE SUN

I gaze into the sun!
I dare
To look at life aflame;
I do not cradle in my arms
The trumpetry of name.

For I was born intense—
A fire—
The world my own to hold;
A bouncing ball to spin at will
In answer to my call.

I hold
No brief for foolish fears;
My knees are strangers to the earth,
I have no need of tears;
For I was born to move erect,
To travel swift and free,
With level look for every man
As God created me. . . .
I gaze into the sun!

IS THIS YOUR SON?

Is this your son he's saving?
Is this your son that saves?
Thank God *they* never stop to ask
"Whose son," these khaki braves.

What though his hair is golden,
What though his face be black;
There's nothing in his soldier-heart
That says, "Don't bring him back!"

But with his uttermost reserves
He gives his fellow aid;
For him he faces death and hell,
Intrepid, unafraid.

Is this your son he's saving?
Is this your son that saves?
God grant the mothers of the earth
Be worthy of their braves.

IN YOUR TREATY

The war, they say, is over,
A new era on its way;
You'll be setting down a treaty,
Making maps of destiny.
And when you draw that treaty
Don't dismiss us with a nod,
Lest you mistake and leave us
On the outside there with God

NEGRO MOTHER PRAYS

Dear God! the sons from my own loins
I send across the sea,
To fight a fight whose ultimate
Lies in obscurity.

To fight a fight for those whose hands
Are cords about their throats,
I'm deeply travailed, wondering
What this event denotes.

Full strong and brave they sally forth
To battle in this war,
And yet, and yet I ask my heart
What are they fighting for?

Oh can it be for manhood-rights
Here in their native land,
Or does it serve some other end
I do not understand?

Whose freedom is it, God, I ask,
Demanding blood of me?
Am I to look at this long last
Upon real liberty?

Or is it that my sons but fight
That other men may be
Reclining in a triumph-car
That we draw heavily?

God grant the day will not be born,
'Twould break my heart to see
My gallant sons returning home
To live on bended knee.

OLD BLACK MEN

They have dreamed, as all men dream,
Of glory, love and power;
They have hoped, as youth will hope,
For life's sun-minted hour;
They have seen, as others saw,
Their visions fade in air;
They have learned to live it down,
As though they did not care.

BLACK WOMAN TURNS AWAY

Don't knock at my door, little child,
    I cannot let you in;
You know not what a world this is
    Of cruelty and sin.
Wait in the still eternity
    Until I come to you;
The world is cruel, cruel, child,
    I cannot let you in!

Don't knock at my heart, little one,
    I cannot bear the pain
Of turning deaf-ear to your call
    Time and time again!
You do not know the monster men
    Inhabiting the earth:
Be still, be still, my precious child,
    I must not give you birth!

ARMAGEDDON

In the silence and the dark
I fought with dragons;
I was battered, beaten sore,
But rose again.
On my knees I fought, still rising,
In my pain;
In the dark I fought with dragons,
But rose again.

Foolish tears
Cease your flowing—
Can't you see the dawn appears!

BLACK RECRUIT

At home, I must be humble, meek,
Surrendering the other cheek;
Must be a coward over here,
And yet a brave man—over there.

This sophistry is passing strange,
Moves quite beyond my mental range;
Since I must be a hero there,
Shall I prepare by crawling here?

Am I a faucet that you turn
To right—I'm cold, to left—I burn!
Or but a golem wound to spring
This way or that—a soulless thing!

He surely is a master-man
Who formulated such a plan.

BLACK BOY'S REQUEST

Just half a chance I ask, not all, but half,
Just half a chance to speed unto the goal,
Just half a chance to qualify a man,
Just half a chance to magnify my soul!

BLACK MAN'S PRAYER

To keep my soul from bitterness
This is my earnest prayer:
To keep the candles of my heart
Aglow and shining there.

Remembering the kindliness
Of all the noble brave,
Who offered up their lives that I
Might cease to be a slave.

But I must reach those gleaming heights
Uncurtained by the dead,
Nor vain shall be the sacrifice
Of precious blood they shed.

To keep my soul from bitterness
This is my earnest prayer:
May all the candles of my heart
Keep bravely burning there.

QUESTION

Where are the brave men,
Where are the strong men?
Pygmies rise
And spawn the earth;
Weak-kneed, weak-hearted, and afraid,
Afraid to face the counsel of their hearts,
Afraid to look men squarely.
Down they gaze,
With fatal fascination,
Down, down
Into the whirling, maggot sands
Of prejudice.

A SONG OF COURAGE

Brave as a lion I must be
To face this jeering world
With my black face and rugged hair;
When every lip is curled
In bald derision as I pass,
A shadow on the looking-glass.

Braver than lions must I be
To give to child of mine
This heritage of certain scorn—
A place among the swine;
And bind him over to the sod
A tethered exile, sorrow-shod.

Braver than all the brave must be
The race of men I bear—
Forged in the furnaces of earth
And wrought to iron there!
The future years have need of them,
I sense it though my sight is dim.

CONQUEST

My pathway lies through worse than death,
I meet the hours with bated breath;
My heart blood boils, my pulses thrill,
I live life running up a hill!

Ah no, I need no paltry play
Of make-shift tilts for holiday;
For I was born against the tide,
And I must conquer things denied.

I shun no hardship, fear no foe,
The future calls and I must go;
I swing to music of the spheres,
As I go fighting down the years!

I CANNOT HATE

I cannot hate—
I have a heart to see,
To feel, to know and understand
Your daring love for me.

True
There are those, a million-fold,
Too blinded yet to see
The primal brotherhood of man
That binds humanity.
They scorn and torture me, deride
And crucify my soul,
But stronger still than them I see
A long, long martyr-roll!

I cannot hate—
This is my song of songs,
I cannot, will not, hate.

V. THE GULF OF CHALLENGE

RICHES

When you count out your gold at the end of the day,
And have winnowed the dross that has cumbered the way;
Oh what were the hold of your treasury then
Save the love you have shown to the children of men?

FOREGATHER

Nor white nor black shall habitate the earth,
But like a rainbow, man shall web and span
The turning globe. The eagle eye may scan
The mingled colours of its living girth—
None may assail the equity of birth.
False values vanish—this shall be the plan,
The mark, the count, the goal to any man
Who runs with courage on the course of earth.

And war shall lift its clutches from the land,
Men shall go forth like children hand in hand,
Vaunting the vision of the recent blind,
Rapt in the vista of the unchained mind.
They shall regather and again recall
The trail lost somewhere since the primal Fall.

CREDO

I believe in the ultimate justice of Fate;
That the races of men front the sun in their turn;
That each soul holds the title to infinite wealth
In fee to the will as it masters itself;
That the heart of humanity sounds the same tone
In impious jungle, or sky-kneeling fane.
I believe that the key to the life-mystery
Lies deeper than reason and further than death.
I believe that the rhythmical conscience within
Is guidance enough for the conduct of men.

HOPE

Frail children of sorrow, dethroned by a hue,
The shadows are checked by the rose sifting through;
The world has its motion, all things pass away,
No night is omnipotent, there must be day.

The oak tarries long in the depth of the seed,
But swift is the season of nettle and weed;
Abide yet awhile in the mellowing shade,
And rise with the hour for which you were made.

The cycle of seasons, the tidals of man,
Revolve in the orb of an infinite plan;
We move to the rhythm of ages long done,
And each has his hour—to dwell in the sun!

THE HIGHEST ART

My heart encircles all the globe,
The proud, the meek, the untoward;
No man stands comfortless outside
My heart—there's room for all inside.

O man of small constricted space—
Expand, fling wide your bounds of grace;
Know that it is the highest art
To take the whole world to your heart.

WITHOUT REASON WHY

Across the ages,
I think of all the proud dead,
Who marched to fatal war
Without reason why.....

Why can't we learn the law of love,
Designed for common-good;
Oh why can't mankind now decide
To live in brotherhood?

I think of all the proud dead
Maturing young for carnage,
Without reason why.....

Why, why, must we hate and slay,
What can we hope to gain?
Can you not see O feeble man
That warfare is in vain?

THE WORD

We say we shall rebuild the world
And make it safe from war;
But first suppose we diagnose
The cause of wars before.

It takes no sage to point the truth—
Down through the ages hurled—
Found in a word, a simple word
To cure an ailing world.

Each nation looked at it askance
Just as we do today;
Decided to have none of it,
And crumbled to decay.

True to his ego, every man
Must play the hero's part;
Feel equal to the other man
Though they be worlds apart.

None may vouchsafe to throttle him
Nor tie his soul around;
For every man is Man's own son,
And earth is common ground.

What is the word, this simple word
With sanctuary curled
Around the earth's remotest rim,
Enclosing all the world?

What is this word so stemmed with life,
Denied, misunderstood?
It is the common blood of man:
The word is—*Brotherhood!*

BROTHERHOOD

Come, Brothers, all!
Shall we not wend
The blind way of our prison world
By sympathy entwined?
Shall we not make
The bleak way for each other's sake
Less rugged and unkind?
O, let each throbbing heart repeat
The faint note of another's beat,
To lift a ballad for the feet
That stumble down life's checkered street!

IMMENSITY

Your world is as big as you make it—
I know for I used to hide
In a narrow nest of earth's corner
My wings folded close to my side.

But I sighted the distant horizon
Where the sky-line circles the sea,
And I was filled with a fierce desire
To breathe this immensity.

I battered the cordons around me,
I cradled my wings on the breeze,
I soared to the furthermost reaches of earth
With power, with rapture, with ease!

TO ONE PREJUDICED

You bluntly say you will not see
Me as your brother man;
Determined not to full admit
Me in your new world plan.

But I who know and understand
Your blindly bitter view,
Will hold the hope that human love
Soon finds its way to you.

THIS HOUR

This is the hour of destiny,
The scales of Time now sway;
Shall we be gathered to the night,
Or see a better day?

TOMORROW

Tomorrow!
Bring to our ken
Surcease from wars and iron heels
Of bitter men.

Inspirit us!
Weary, worn with worlds of yesterday.
Show valleys of simple peace,
And quiet joy
In quiet things.

YOU CANNOT HATE THE MAN YOU KNOW

You Cannot Hate the Man You Know—
You'll find this adage true;
A certain sympathy is born
When men draw close to you.

You only hate the thing that's strange,
The man who dwells apart;
But none can ever know and hate
Another human heart.

BUILD BRIDGES EVERYWHERE

Let's build bridges here and there,
Or sometimes just a spiral stair,
That we may come somewhat abreast
And sense what cannot be express't;
For by these measures can be found
A meeting place, a common ground
Nearer the reaches of the heart
Where truth revealed, stands clear, apart;
With understanding come to know
What laughing lips will never show,
How tears and torturing distress
May masquerade as happiness;
Then you will know when my heart's aching,
And I, when yours is slowly breaking!

Oh, let's build bridges everywhere,
And span the gulf of challenge there!

EVENTUALLY AT NIGHTFALL

Yes
Finally
'Twill come to this
The rock-ribbed primal truth
Mankind shall come together
After travail and ruth.

When throbbing veins yield up their blood
And terror stalks the earth
Man shall perceive the mockery
Of scaling mortal birth.

Yes
Someday
In the eventide
Before night's final fall
Poor blinded humankind will see
We're brothers—after all!

RESOLUTION

With but one life full certified,
And that of every gleam denied
My portion;
Close to the unrelenting sod,
Even as my fathers dumbly trod,
I've slumbered;
But now a surging, wild unrest
Uproots the poppies from my breast,
My soul awake, erect, anew,
I stand and face the star-swept blue,
And swear to make my dreams come true!

PUBLICATIONS OF THE STUART A. ROSE
MANUSCRIPT, ARCHIVES, AND RARE BOOK
LIBRARY AT EMORY UNIVERSITY

Emory as Place: Meaning in a University Landscape
by Gary S. Hauk

Dear Regina: Flannery O'Connor's Letters from Iowa
edited by Monica Carol Miller

After a Thousand Tears: Poems
by Georgia Douglass Johnson, edited and
with a new introduction by Jimmy Worthy II